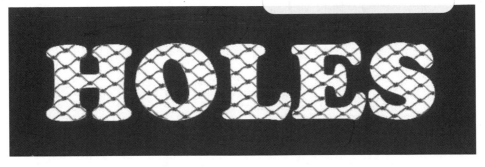

HOLES

Scotland's Salmon Sewage Scandal

by

James Merryweather

PRE-PUBLICATION EDITION

Specially prepared for the community of Sleat, Isle of Skye.

Hurriedly prepared to coincide with planning applications for three fish farms intended for Lochs Slapin and Eishort, Isle of Skye.

[the finished edition will be published once the dust has settled]

Blue-Skye Books

2014

Blue-Skye BOOKS

http://www.blue-skye.org.uk

Published 2014 by Blue-Skye Books
Auchtertyre, Scotland, IV40 8EG U.K.
james@blue-skye.org.uk

Temporary ISBN 13: 978-1500800260

RATIONALE

HOLES is part of a community effort to protect the south Skye sea lochs

Loch Scavaig, Loch Slapin & Loch Eishort

from unsympathetic industrial development and shameless pollution.

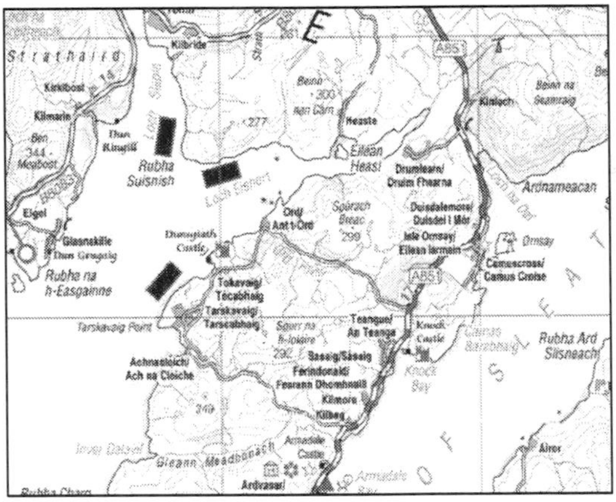

By the same author

York Music (1988). York, Sessions.

Merryweather's Tunes for the English Bagpipe (1989). Newbiggin, Dragonfly.

The Fiddler of Helperby (1994). Newbiggin, Dragonfly.

The Fern Guide 3rd ed. (2007). Shrewsbury, Field Studies Council.

A Key To Common Ferns (2005). Shrewsbury, Field Studies Council.

Dr Merryweather's Song-Booke (2005). Mytholmroyd, Ruxbury.

Reality is Enough(2013). Blue-Skye Books.

User-Friendly Seashore Guide (2013). Blue-Skye Books.

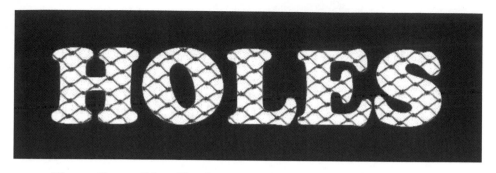

HOLES

Scotland's Salmon Sewage Scandal

Contents

"The salmon farming industry pays nothing for waste disposal. Fish faeces go directly into the ocean. Our environment and wild marine species pay the price that secures the industry's profits." – Living Oceans

PREFACE

> Mrs. Pants (house buyer): But what about the privies?
>
> Blackadder: Um, well, what we are talking about in privy terms is the latest in front wall fresh air orifices combined with a wide capacity gutter installation below.
>
> Mrs. Pants: You mean you *crap* out the window?
>
> Blackadder: Yes.
>
> Blackadder II episode 4: *Money* (1986)

Ordure

The Blackadder scene is good fun and a fitting illustration here, but I'm not sure anybody ever routinely crapped straight out of the window, even *in those days*. It is unthinkable even that we should (as people surely used to do) casually tip wet waste – ugh, surely not the contents of a chamber pot? – out of an upstairs window into the street accompanied by a merry, if badly timed: "Gardyloo!"

Just think though:

- A thousand tonnes of horse dung dumped daily in the London streets is a thing of the past, pretty well forgotten.
- Pet owners are obliged to scoop up and dispose of their dogs' dirt in the bin provided or take it home – preferably not decorate the bushes with bags of muck or snag them along a barbed-wire fence.
- How do you feel when, with its owner's blessing, a dog leaves its calling card on the pavement?
- When disgusted seaside bathers complain about turds bobbing in the water (it really happened to me once, at Bridlington – Yeeugh!), swimming is instantly forbidden and the polluter called to account.
- In what we call 'the civilised world', human excrement is treated in high-tech sewage farms or septic tanks to make it sweet and safe, ready for decent disposal.

There is one exception to these reasonable, civilised rules. Net-cage fish farms dump *all* of their fish excrement, from as many as a million salmon per farm, entirely untreated, straight into the sea, twenty-four/seven.

Allow me to emphasise that:

A major industry – open-cage aquaculture – is allowed to dispose of all its raw sewage, directly into the sea, in spite of predictable environmental detriment and at no cost whatsoever to the polluter.

If you watch only one YouTube video about salmon farming, please watch the one that includes this brief but poignant passage in its commentary.[1] This pretty well says it all:

> "One reason net-cage industrial farming is profitable is due to externalised costs. At present the salmon farming industry pays nothing for waste disposal. Fish faeces and uneaten feed pellets go directly into the ocean. Our environment and wild marine species pay the price that secures the industry's profits." – Living Oceans[2]

Imagine you have an aquarium with no filtration system (or even with). If you do, you will have first-hand experience of this. What happens after a while? The water becomes foul and the tank needs cleaning out. Why? Because fishes do what all animals do, they defecate – profusely. To micro-organisms faeces makes a delicious meal and they joyfully eat and reproduce, fouling the water in your tank and, if you don't do something about it, killing its occupants.

Imagine a similar situation, but with instead of a few goldfish in a tank, fifty to ninety thousand fully grown salmon confined to a cage sitting in the sea. Alright, the tide sloshes in and out helping to disperse the fish droppings, but where does it all go? What effect does it have on fish farm surroundings? In view of our fish tank experience it's probably not good. Does it break down to harmless stuff and simply wash away, of no further concern?

In western Scotland, where most 'British' or 'Scottish' fish farms are located (you will understand the inverted commas later – Chapter 3), there are around a hundred and fifty-seven salmon farms active at any one time,[3] each consisting of ten or twelve cages, making the total number of farmed salmon in Scotland – back-of-an-envelope calculation – approximately a hundred million – all defecating in the sea. That's a lot of dung, not entirely dissimilar to all those Victorian horse bus horses dumping on the streets of London, perhaps worse:

> "This year [2000], salmon farms will produce 7,500 tons of nitrogen, equivalent to the annual sewage from 3.2 million people, and 1,240 tons of phosphorus, comparable to sewage from 9.4 million people. The ecological result is effectively greater than the sewage produced by Scotland's 5.1 million humans." – Dr Malcolm MacGarvin[4]

Solid organic[5] material from dispersing salmon faeces settles and accumulates on the sea bed whilst finer sediments and dissolved chemical waste are dispersed by tides and currents. Near or far? Diluted safely to extinction? Who knows? Well, apparently the authorities do, the Scottish Environment Protection Agency (SEPA) in particular, and surprisingly they generally approve. Quantities and impacts are predicted by

---

1 http://www.youtube.com/watch?v=qYCEGtMdORU
2 www.livingoceans.org
3 According to Scott Landsburgh (Scottish Salmon Producers Organisation) interviewed on Countryfile, BBC1, 1 Dec. 2013. "Two hundred and fifty seven farms of which about a hundred and fifty seven active at any given time."
4 Quoted by *Telegraph* columnist Charles Clover, author of book and film concerned about overfishing The End of the Line.
http://www.telegraph.co.uk/news/uknews/1355936/Pollution-from-fish-farms-as-bad-as-sewage.html
5 Organic is word that can convey the wrong meaning if we are not careful. Here it is used in the sense of chemical compounds derived from living matter and containing carbon in their formula.

modelling, but contrary to the views of the regulators, I contend that ecological impacts cannot fully be determined, even after the event, because the biology of the seas has yet to be properly understood. Indications are that sewage is not good for the marine environment (to put it mildly).

Therefore, I maintain a healthy scepticism about government rules laid down by regulatory authorities that are responsible to governments who, in their turn, are politicians (not biologists) whose decisions might be influenced by commercial and economic concerns as well as the ballot box.

Once upon a time we humans presumed that fish stocks were so vast that fishing could never dent their capacity for population recovery. We were utterly wrong: Overfishing has landed us and the fishes in deep trouble.[6] With the same know-all attitude, we have been throwing all sorts of waste out to sea for a long time, massively over the past two hundred years, assuming it will be diluted to extinction. That works only in homeopathy![7]

What makes us think that because, seen from our terrestrial viewpoint, Scottish waters are lovely and clean and the sea is big, we can carry on as usual, allowing the aquaculture industry to dispose of all its sewage in the sea lochs? For very sensible, well understood reasons individual householders are not allowed to do it, so why a whole industry of fish-farmers?

A Rude Word – No Apologies

Let's make it crystal clear and get the initial shock over with: Speaking frankly, this book is about fish shit. Yes, there are more delicate ways of putting it, but I'm not going to ask you to 'pardon my French'.

The problem is so serious that it's worth giving the reader an encouraging little jolt of indignation by saying a minor obscenity right at the start. If it upsets you, take comfort by imagining Cissie and Ada (Les Dawson and Roy Barraclough) mouthing the naughty word silently to one another and you might find it gives less offence.

When I give talks about fish farming I usually slip in this outrageous four-letter word just once – accompanying a slide showing a dog turd so realistic you can almost smell it – just to assure the audience that what we're considering is unseen pollution that is widespread, revolting and dangerous. It's not just a minor inconvenience and it's something of concern to us all, not just a few precious environmentalists, NIMBYs and sea-huggers.

Anyway, the word is not considered so terribly rude these days, but it still packs a bit of a punch. If I could have got away with it, this book's title might have been just plain *FISH SHIT*, short, snappy and very much to the point, a very effective come-and-buy-me 'hook' don't you think? It would stand out among the best-sellers placed enticingly on tables set in the entrance to every chain bookstore.

---

6 Clover, C. (2005). The End Of The Line: How overfishing is changing the world and what we eat. Ebury Press.

7 And just to make sure my point is clear: Homeopathy does not work. http://www.nhs.uk/conditions/homeopathy/Pages/Introduction.aspx

Who is Likely to Read HOLES?

The first consideration was this would be a publication for the enlightenment of the Sleat (Skye) community. We have tackled two fish farm planning applications which threaten to make a mess of an exceptional landscape and marine environment, and arguably the livelihoods of several groups of local people. We have two more to go, plus a veritable assault of others in the region, and if we are to succeed in keeping a classic landscape clear of industrial indignities, the momentum must be maintained.

This book is, if you like, a non-trivial gimmick, intended to promote community understanding of a difficult topic which a few of us have the privilege of being just a jump or two ahead of the rest, and encourage people to engage with the consultation process each and every time. Next we will have to catch the interest of the people of Sleat once more and then, later, we will have to do it again. We really need creative ideas that will draw people in and encourage them to take part in two more consultations as well as any aftermath if the fish farm people don't like the council's verdicts (assuming they take notice of public opinion – Chapter 10).

I hope you can see that our purpose is not to tell people what they should think or do, rather to inform and engage: information, not indoctrination. [They can get any amount of the latter elsewhere.]

However, our aspirations extend beyond the borders of the south Skye peninsula and its adjacent sea lochs. We are now persuaded that net-cage salmon farming is out-of-date and detrimental in most respects wherever installed in clean open water, and that it can relatively easily be made environmentally safe. That last requires either willing adaptation by aquaculturalists and/or stern direction by law that they must clean up or get out.

We intend that this book should be widely available, especially in western Scotland where such knowledge as we have accrued can be made available to others: to save them the time, mistakes and head-scratching we have already had to invest as we ascended a steep learning curve. We hope that the Community Councils in all coastal communities affected by fish farming will want to join in and make salmon farming a clean and *truly* sustainable industry. First we must stand in the way of new farms and then get them to change their ways and clean up existing installations.

Author's Motivation

I am a half-and-half person. I have always been equally enthusiastic about both music and science, not as a a mere spectator, but always an actively participating practitioner. I have been an orchestral bassoon player and performer of medieval and renaissance music and at the same time a biologist with a wide array of interests, general and specialised. Science-wise, if I must be labelled, any one of biologist, natural historian or naturalist will do. So my involvement in the fish farm controversy is an emergent property of my concern for the safety of nature and landscape, because they are at the centre of my life-long passion. My attachment to nature does not involve the accumulation of money. If only! Sometimes I wish it did (even just a little bit), but profit or wealth are not the reason for being a biologist. It's sheer fascination, innate or absorbed at a very early age and inextinguishable. A lot of people don't get the same kicks out of life as a congenital biologist.

I was once taken completely off balance during a fish farms talk I presented in Ullapool, way up north in western Scotland. Having outlined my biological credentials and compared my vested interests – none – with those whose jobs or fortunes depend upon fish farming, I was surprised into stumbling silence when one questioner wanted to know who I was working for, which organisation I represented – essentially who was paying me to be there that evening.

My inability to answer was due to my innocently not comprehending the question or the interrogator's purpose in asking. I suspected nothing and eventually replied truthfully that I was not being paid and, in answer to the next question, that the expenses for the event came out of my own pocket. The meeting then proceeded because the questioner then had no response to an altruistic gesture that quite obviously involved a lot of expertise, hard work and expense. Without affectation, I had appeared genuinely innocent and the other was dumfounded by the very idea of somebody appearing on behalf of a cause for no remuneration.

As I told that audience: Having to go about the country defending biology rather than *doing* biology is an annoying waste of my time. I don't want to be forced into fighting for my subject. I want to be out there enjoying it. I listed the reasons and non-reasons for my anti-fish farm stance. First I emphasised the NOes (which are obviously not applicable to anyone who is anti fish farms), then listed the YESes and ended with just one that best describes me and my motives and that also matters most to me: Biologist.

Financial Gain: NO	Conservationist: YES
Income Dependent: NO	'Environmentalist': If you must
Employment Dependent: NO	NIMBY: Isn't everybody?
Fish-Farm Employee: NO	Teacher: YES
Fish-Farm Shareholder: NO	Community Outreach: YES
Fish-Farming Expert: NO	Pursuit of Happiness: YES
Eco-Warrior: NO	**Biologist: YES**
Tree-Hugger: Not really	

I also confidently stated that:

Since my views are not affected by employment or income,

I am *allowed* to hold contrary opinions, with no job at risk.

I am *free* to use all of the evidence to reach my own honest opinions ... and also *free* to change my mind.

I am independent, so my opinions will be objective.

I did a lot of thinking when devising those few slides and edited them many, many times before I was satisfied. I claimed that my vested interests were zero, unless of course they wished to count my life-long passion for natural history. I emphasised the bleak contrast of that attitude with the mostly financial interests of fish farm employees (out in force that evening and spoiling for a rumble) and their wealthy bosses, most of them in luxurious offices far away in Norway. The audience had nothing to say about all that until later, when they wanted to know who was paying me to be there. In their minds, if it wasn't money, I *had* to have some sneaky motive, my own vested interest, and they were determined to expose it. They couldn't.

Of course, I agree with the barrister's dictum that: "A vested interest doesn't mean that evidence is untrue."[8] but I maintain that untrue evidence is very poor evidence (it's not evidence at all), and an opinion based on untrue evidence must be just plain wrong. The few of us who notice when the aquaculture industry promulgates 'evidence' that we can detect has been 'adjusted' have the responsibility of pointing it out to everybody else, allowing them to reach their own fair judgement.

On the other hand, we who protest about fish farming must make sure the evidence we use in our case is true, so that our opinions may be plausible and trustworthy. Put another way: If we want to be right, we should say only what we know to be true. For people like us, that's a much easier strategy than contrived deception, which we can leave to others.

Fishy Note

Some readers will be perplexed by my use of two related plural words that are apparently interchangeable or at least one is right and the other is wrong: 'fishes' and 'fish'. Many years ago, for a while, I was troubled wondering which should one use in which context, until I discussed it with my friend 'Bone' (who is very wise about many matters, including what the fish bones, gut parasite eggs and sloe stones found in human coprolites tell archaeologists about the diets of past civilisations) and read what the renowned ichthyologist Alwynne Wheeler had to say on the subject. I was delighted that their advice was unequivocal – *you* might say pedantic (but I don't care; not as much as I care about correct use of English).

Fishes means live or dead whole fishes of
single or mixed species as found in the water.

Fish means dead individuals and fillets
thereof as displayed on the fish monger's slab.

8 Sir Desmond de Silva, QC on BBC R4 Today, 21 Jan. 2014.

Acknowledgements

Since October 2012 a number of people have accepted the task of working and learning so that we may protect the South Skye Lochs from industrial harm. As I saw it happen, it all began when Eileen Armstrong of Ord saw the need for action and contacted a number of us to see who could assist her. She has remained steadfast and hard working on the project ever since, though – like the rest of us – sometimes weary of annoying distractions from a comfortable life such as fish farms, which in an ideal world would never trouble us.

Biologists on the team include Roger Cottis whose main (far from only) expertise is with mammals. Roger and I have performed our *Fish Farm Roadshow* several times, I as front man with the PowerPoint show and Roger as chairman keeping order with his bell.

Arthur Sevestre, who has a particularly innovative interest in maintaining an unspoilt environment, has been involved in many discussions and events and maintains an informative if individualistic anti-fish farming website, Skye Marine Concern[9].

As secretary of Sleat Community Council, Rob Ware maintains a rigorously neutral stance whilst being our link with the Sleat community, letting everyone know what is going on when fish farm plans are afoot.

Others who played significant and varied roles are Skye & Lochalsh Environment Forum, David Ashford, Roddy Murray, Annabel Pendlebury, Duncan Steedman, Iain Turnbull and Alex Turner.

---

9 www.skyemarineconcern.org

Chapter 1

UP WITH THIS WE WILL NOT PUT

"The wild, crashing seas create the perfect environment in which to rear the very best fish.[10] Our farms are located in the wide open sea[11] where the strong tidal currents of the North Sea and the North Atlantic Ocean meet, creating a powerful water exchange that not only provides fast-flowing clear water and maintains a clean seabed,[12] but also provides a natural habitat for salmon to swim against the tide[13] developing the strongest and healthiest of fish."[14] – Hjaltland Seafood[15]

Sewage, Ecology & Truth

Even the best marine scientists – they won't mind me saying this – have a frustratingly poor understanding of multi-trophic[16] food webs[17] and complexes of symbiotic species. Symbiosis[18] involves *all* organisms and *all* habitats, and what scientists have found out about the ecology of symbiosis assures us that we know lamentably little about how interlinked species interact and how communities of interlinked species function. Indeed, all of these phenomena, about which the general public is almost entirely unaware, constitute the foundations upon which ecological communities depend for their existence.

How can anyone, scientist or lay person, especially with industrial concerns who would rather not bother about such irritations which interfere with the conduct of their businesses,[19] predict how ecosystems will respond to damaging influences until such complex ecological intricacies are fully understood? Damage to them causes problems we never notice until, perhaps, major detrimental changes becomes undeniably apparent. Often the most obscure, invisible or even undetectable species[20] or most complicated ecological processes can be fundamental to the integrity of habitats, which may collapse even when a single component is perturbed. Usually, we have no

---

10 Wild, crashing seas also destroy fish farms with dire consequences for aquaculture and wild fish stocks: http://www.bbc.co.uk/news/uk-scotland-north-east-orkney-shetland-26459825

11 Sheltered Scottish lochs are wide open sea?

12 Really?

13 Round and round, languidly, in a perpetual corporate gyration.

14 Wild salmon tend to be the strongest and healthiest unless infested with sea lice, concentrated on salmon in the fish farms they have to swim past during migrations – see Chapter 5.

15 http://www.shetland-products.com/index.php/en/farming/overview

16 Involving species of different feeding levels in a food chain.

17 http://en.wikipedia.org/wiki/Food_web

18 Two or more species living in a close association, usually with benefits for the association and/or its components.

19 They don't want to know, or waste time on such trivia, except insofar as they are obliged to by the regulatory authorities, and then they contribute as little as they can get away with. Profit routinely trumps environment (Chapter 10).

20 Probably the majority of life on earth has yet to be detected.

idea when such catastrophes are happening or – because we lack realistic baseline data – that they have already happened until after the damage has been done and realistic attempts at restoration are impossible (because we don't know what was there before we destroyed it).

We *do* know that sea bed flora and fauna can be severely affected (in many cases fatally) by sedimentation[21] and eutrophication[22] caused by unrestricted release and deposition of fish farm effluent. Sea bed community structure becomes drastically simplified and only a minority of organisms thrive beneath or in the vicinity of a fish farm, such as the rampant filamentous bacterium *Beggiatoa* that feeds on sulphur, and ravenous muck-eating worms called *Capitella.* Fish farms cause severe, perhaps catastrophic, reductions in biodiversity, certainly locally and probably more subtly on a wider scale.

> ***N.B. Published scientific literature contains a lot of evidence of ecological detriment caused by fish farms and absolutely NONE demonstrating neutral impact or ecological improvement (whatever that might be).***

Nevertheless, aquaculture spokespersons often blithely claim, without producing a scrap of evidence, that their fish farms are harmless or even – can you believe it? – that they might actually benefit the marine environment.

> "Our method of farming has very little impact on the seabed ... and we leave a fish farm site in at least as good a status as it was and we often do much to rejuvenate sites, and leave them better than we found them."
>
> – Craig Anderson, Scottish Salmon Company[23]

This is, of course, untrue. If it warrants it, a spade must be called a spade, so that is what I must call this: untrue (= a lie). I'm afraid I will probably have to write or hint at these unfortunate concepts again as this book progresses (the reader may translate them into less polite alternatives according to taste), but we sometimes witness spokespersons saying things they might wish they hadn't, or what their employers instruct them to say, or – *how shall I put this?* – what they truly believe to be so, when it can be shown to be not so. The future of fish farming, which they refer to *ad nauseam* as a 'sustainable[24] industry', and the jobs of those employed on fish farms depend upon public confidence that aquaculture is a benign activity.[25] Industry spokespersons' jobs depend upon presenting the public with their company's line, which sometimes is – *how shall I put this?* – not necessarily fully in accord with reality. Here is an example:

---

21 Smothering by a rain of fine particles.

22 Chemical enrichment, which overfeeds a minority of greedy species that flourish at the expense of biodiversity.

23 http://www.fishupdate.com/

24 Weasel Word Warning: Sustainable is used in two conflicting ways, allowed by some users to overlap imperceptibly while the listener is not fully attending: 1. Economic. Sustainable growth; 2. Environmental. Capable of being maintained at a steady level without exhausting natural resources or causing detrimental ecological change.

25 I know from my own personal change of mind about salmon farming in October 2012 that such beliefs can be dashed in pieces in a short while by the application of genuine knowledge.

Countryfile[26] presenter Tom Heap first interviewed Andrew Graham-Stewart, whose responsibilities are wild Salmon and Trout, and then Scott Landsburgh, the main fish farms spokesman in Scotland:

> Tom Heap: "In Scotland alone [fish-farming is] worth five hundred and thirty-seven million pounds and employs over two thousand people, but despite its growth and its economic success, it still is highly controversial. Upstream in Glen Coe I'm starting to find out why."
>
> Andrew Graham-Stewart: "Twenty-five years ago, the local angling club counted five hundred salmon in this one pool, just downstream of here. Today if you counted five you'd be very lucky."
>
> TH: "Andrew Graham-Stewart from the Salmon and Trout Association of Scotland fears for the future of wild fish as a result of fish-farming. So what is causing this collapse?"
>
> AG-S: "The problem is sea lice, sea lice from the fish-farms. They're a small parasite and they live [on] and eat the flesh of salmonids; salmon and sea trout."
>
> TH: "But sea lice do occur naturally in the ocean, don't they?"
>
> AG-S: "They do. There's a natural background level of sea lice in the sea, but fish-farms ... when you've got half a million fish or so in the fish-farms ... there's a reservoir of breeding adults which create billions, literally billions of sea lice larvae, which spread out into the sea lochs and you've then got what is called a sea lice soup through which the juvenile fish, which aren't adapted to coping with those numbers of lice, have got to swim. The latest credible study, which was done by sea lice experts from Scotland, Canada and Norway, concluded that thirty-four percent of salmon leaving these rivers next to fish-farms die as a result."
>
> ---
>
> TH (to camera): "Andrew says that fish-farms and the lice they generate push down the numbers of salmon in rivers like this on the west coast of Scotland to an all-time low and he also says the industry is not acknowledging its part in creating this problem. So, what does the Scottish Salmon Producers' Organisation [SSPO] have to say about that?"
>
> ---
>
> TH (interview): "Scott, are lice from your farms killing wild salmon?"
>
> Scott Landsburgh: "No. I wouldn't say so. I mean, there's a lot of discussion about it but ... um ... there's no empirical evidence that suggests that that's the case."
>
> TH: "Why, then, does the industry spend millions of pounds each year on chemicals to treat lice?"

---

26 BBC1, 1 December 2013.

SL: "er ... we ... we want to ensure ... a ... that we have healthy fish. I mean, y'know, y'know, that's the key to our future. We ... we want to have a sustainable industry here. It's a challenge, but it's a challenge for wild fish and it's a challenge for farmed fish as well."[27]

TH: "So, you acknowledge it's a challenge ..."

SL: "Yeah."

TH: "... so are you taking at least some responsibility for making sure that you reduce the lice burden out there?"

SL: "er ... Oh yes, but I mean, as I said .. er ... the, the parasite starts in the wild and we obviously have to manage the challenge that comes to the fish-farm."[28]

TH: "Concerns have been raised about the environmental impacts of these anti-lice chemicals. In a recent three-year study of the main fish-farming areas in Scotland more than nine percent of the sea bed samples exceeded environmental standards. The SSPO says it's working to reduce chemicals in salmon farms."

The spokesman for wild fishes claims they are harmed by fish farming and the spokesman for the fish farms denies it. To my mind, "No" (which *was* Landsburgh's reply) is as unequivocal as a denial can get. So who is right? Is somebody not telling the truth? Somebody's gotta be right and somebody's gotta be wrong – when the answer is a straight yes or no there can be no ifs or buts. What does science have to say on the matter? Here's what Marine Scotland Science (Scottish Government advisors) wrote in their official comment in the consultation regarding a fish farm planning application in June 2014:[29]

- Are salmon farms a significant source of lice? Yes,
- Is there an association between levels of lice on salmon farms and in the surrounding environment? Yes,
- Is there an association between levels of lice on salmon farms and on sea trout? Yes,
- Is there an effect of sea lice on wild trout at the individual level? Yes,
- Is there an effect of sea lice on wild salmon at the population level? Experiments undertaken in Norway and Ireland have shown that sea lice caused a loss of on average 39% of adult salmon recruitment (Krkosek *et al.* in press).[30]

Need I say more?

I will.

---

27 As far as I can tell, this last sentence contributes nothing to the discussion. It's meaningless.

28 ... where the sea louse infestation gets massively concentrated on the captive fishes and then re-infests the wild fish community in much greater numbers than before.

29 http://wam.highland.gov.uk/wam/applicationDetails.do?activeTab=documents&keyVal=N3VEIBIH09K00

30 Also see Chapter 5.

Aquaculture spokespersons also routinely remind everyone that fish farming is governed by and obeys limitations laid down and policed by government managed authorities, such as Marine Scotland (MS), the Scottish Environment Protection Agency (SEPA) and Scottish Natural Heritage (SNH). Some do try to conform, but demonstrably, fish farms have been known to flout official guidelines. May I draw your attention to the 'satisfactory' records of Wester Ross Fisheries Ltd. and Loch Duart ('the Sustainable Salmon Company').

Graph 2: SEPA fish-farm benthic reports by classification and by company

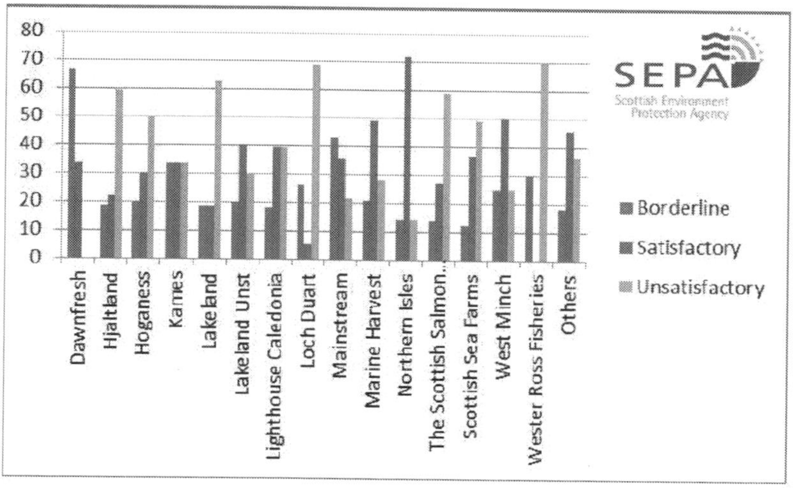

Organic Pollution of the sea bed under fish-farms in Scottish Sea Lochs 2009 – 2011
[Salmon & Trout Association report, August 2012[31]]

Statutory limitations on fish farm effluent were devised when fish farms were relatively small and relatively few, when fish farm effluent was generally considered to be slight, benign. Now that we appreciate that fish farms are net polluters,[32] the rules on pollution can be seen to be inadequate and in need of a complete overhaul. And I mean complete: pulling fish-farms out onto land and using tanks in place of those poo-leaky nets.

Up with this we *can* put

Net-cage aquaculture is an outmoded practice already superseded by closed-containment and combined aquaculture-hydroponic systems (Chapter 8) that eliminate all the disadvantages of open nets (except one). No more sea lice, faeces and waste food pollution, chemical pesticide pollution (e.g. SLICE™ Emamectin Benzoate and its metabolic derivatives), approach of predatory mammals, harm to vulnerable birds, fish escapes, genetic mixing (farmed *vs.* wild) and crashing wild fish populations. Add

---

31 Guy Linley-Adams (2012). Organic pollution of the sea-bed under fish-farms in Scottish sea lochs 2009-2011. Salmon & Trout Association, Scotland. Y axis shows percentage of total sea bed condition reports. http://www.salmon-trout.org/pdf/S&TA_Report_organic_pollution_report_August_2012.pdf

32 This was not intended to be pun, but it is one. Read on and you will soon get it.

to all those that the product has firmer flesh (like wild fish) and there's no more need to dye pallid meat salmon-coloured.

Repeat: Closed-containment aquaculture eliminates all ecological disadvantages of open nets.[33]

The single disadvantage of aquaculture, as currently practiced, not accounted for by closed-containment is the significant percentage of fish in feed pellets. Salmon are top predators and cannot be forced into vegetarianism or expected to make do with a piscine junk food diet. They need solid, oily meat to eat. They need to feed on what they catch in the wild: other fishes. So their diet must include at least some fish, which means sardines, capelin, anchovies and similar oily fish, hoovered out of the sea in ever increasing quantities to the detriment of wild fish stocks, marine ecosystems and people who rely on them for their own sustenance.

Work is proceeding on replacing fish with meat consisting of lots of king ragworm *Alitta virens*, easily produced artificially and without recourse to harvesting natural populations.[34]

How and why did HOLES come into existence?

This book emerged from an urgent community effort. With only two weeks before the consultation would close, the people of Sleat, at the south end of the Isle of Skye in the Scottish Inner Hebrides, received notice that a company called Marine Harvest had applied for planning permission to install a fish farm in Loch Slapin. It was by sheer chance that somebody got wind of it because the powers that be had decided that Sleat was not adjacent to Loch Slapin and, therefore, did not constitute an interested community. Justifiably, Sleat thought otherwise, but the few people who had heard of what they thought might be an imminent threat to their environment had absolutely no idea what to do. They didn't really know whether or not a fish farm constituted an environmental or any other sort of threat.

Locals began talking to one another, and this author – who does not live on Skye, but close by and visits the area frequently – was contacted seeking his biological assistance. After a tense hiatus, I got to appreciate the problem and replied saying I'd do what little I could to advise on a subject about which I knew nothing. In fact, in a passive, vacuous, non-reasoning way, I thought fish farming was probably a good idea because it ought to reduce pressure on over exploited wild fish stocks. How wrong I was: something I soon came to realise when mounting the steep learning curve now required of me.

I joined a small group of concerned *Sgitheanachs*[35] assembled to discuss what should be done. We were all thoroughly aware that any project we might feel obliged to embark upon would take up time we could not afford to spend on it, as well as our massive ignorance of the subject. These would become burdens to carry for years,

---

33 Apart from fish in fish feed, see Chapter 9.

34 http://www.allaboutfeed.net/Process-Management/Management/2009/11/Ragworms-show-promise-as-substitute-for-fish-meal-AAF011454W/; http://www.theguardian.com/environment/2012/dec/17/scottish-salmon-fishing

35 The name for Skye inhabitants in the local tongue, Gaelic.

sharing them with one another for support at times when we felt too downhearted to keep going.

The internet was searched. People in other parts of the West Highlands dealing with the same problem (many!) were contacted and even a few from abroad in Norway and Canada were consulted. Documents were saved, printed and shared among us and we talked and talked. In two weeks we learnt an immense amount, but not enough to feel satisfied we could successfully stand up to the might of big business. With what knowledge we did have, we gathered the community and told them about it, hoping some of them would assist us with the task of commenting in the public consultation that was already under way when we first heard about the proposed new fish farm.

They did! For:Against a new fish farm 1:75. At least the public part of the consultation had shown overwhelming disapproval among the public. The quality of objection was very mixed, too many submissions pedantically personal: "I don't like it" or less than well-informed. No complaints, because we had rallied honest support, but we could tell that next time – we knew a next time would soon be upon us – we would have to share our recently accumulated understanding of the subject around the community so they could write with greater authority founded on knowledge.

One aspect of that first application we encountered had us utterly baffled. Marine Harvest did not have an option on the Crown Estates lease on the Loch Slapin site. This was public knowledge, easily found out, so why were they proceeding with their bid? We still don't understand this and can only speculate that there was some business-political strategy behind it.

Interestingly, something equally odd is going on in another Skye sea loch system, Loch Snizort (location of nearby Uig, the Skye port for ferries to the Outer Hebrides). In 2012, Marine Harvest applied for planning at a site known as Snizort South. Shortly after, Hjaltland began preparations for planning permission at three sites, Snizort East, Snizort West and ... Snizort South. Before acceptance or rejection, Marine Harvest withdrew their application and Hjaltland stepped into their place, with a full proposal for Snizort East, the other two in preparation.

At Loch Slapin more-or-less the same happened: Marine Harvest, the applicant, pulled out just days before the planners' decision and very soon Hjaltland formally applied to occupy the same site with two other planning applications for fish farms in adjacent Loch Eishort in prep. A possible explanation for their pulling out – apart from no site lease and unfathomable politicking – was that the Highland Council's planning committee was about to recommend refusal of the application because the proposal contravened several local planning policies. After all the expense and effort of preparing a planning application (not so great, but read on) it still seems odd that they should have withdrawn at the eleventh hour.

Our bemused conclusion: Political shenanigans that are incomprehensible to lay persons, even if they are moderately intelligent and wary.

At the time of writing, the public consultation for Hjaltland's Loch Slapin bid has just closed. It is too early to determine the final pro:con balance (currently 2:65, which looks promising) but since their chosen site is within a whisker of being precisely Marine Harvest's, which before withdrawal was to be rejected on planning grounds, we naïve members of the public expect it to be rejected for the same reasons and will want to know why not if it passes. Will we have any say in the matter? (See Chapter 10.)

Planning Inequalities (but also see end of chapter: STOP PRESS)

Will we be allowed to have our say? You see, this draws our attention to some annoying differences between the rights of us the public and those enjoyed by the industry and the authorities. After the first consultation we had the dubious pleasure of experiencing, certain of us were led to understand (instructed in almost scolding terms) that if we thought we could just send in the same letter of objection next time, we could think again. If recognised, it would likely be overlooked. As it happens, with the second application for the same site in the same loch by a different company, the same objections applied, so that condition might have proved somewhat unfair except that this time we had learnt immensely more about the subject, so we wanted to write brand new objection letters anyway.

However, this is one of three unfairnesses in the consultation system. A scan of one applicant's documents shows them to have been compiled from their a previously submitted application for another site, more-or-less by copy and paste, and then edited to suit. A prime example that caught my eye was a sentence in such bad English I had already failed to untangle when it first appeared had been copied exactly word-for-word in the echoing 'new' document:

> "Conclusions. Through careful site selection, management and following best practice the potential impacts on the environment will be minimised as can be reasonably foreseen."

Many text passages in these applications are either meaningless or incomprehensible. This one I suspect is an example of both. It's not conclusions, it's gobbledegook! Spelling and grammatical errors also got transferred *verbatim* from one application to the next. Also, it has now transpired, one of the hydrographic reports contained irrelevant data from a previous application, not updated in the applicant's haste. That was a bit obvious, though it slipped past most scrutineers.

It is plain that, while the fish farm companies – who have the staff and finance to deal with research and paperwork – may submit the same or similar (often extremely poorly presented) documents, edited to suit each case, the public – whose experience, time and resources are woefully limited because they already have full lives to lead – may not.

The second unfairness: The public must adhere to a closing date, after which no more correspondence will be entertained by the planning office. However, official responses may and do arrive after *our* closing date making it impossible for us to comment on late submissions. That might be important, particularly when we disagree with opinions expressed by Marine Scotland, SNH or SEPA, who are supposed to represent our interests. This has indeed occurred in the recently closed Loch Slapin consultation, so a protest will be lodged.

The third unfairness is that, after consultation the public will be allowed no further part in the planning process; no opportunity to discuss outcomes. However, if a fish farm company is dissatisfied with the planning officers' decision, it has right of appeal. So, if an application is allowed through in spite of contraventions of any, in our experience often *many* considerations, nobody may speak up and contest errors. As far as I know, a dissatisfied fish farm company could appeal to a higher authority, for instance the Scottish Government, and likely to get a local council's decision overturned.

As you might be able to see now, we once highly inexperienced locals have learnt a great deal since the emergency of October 2012. It takes time and tries our patience severely, but eventually irregularities in the planning process do become apparent to us and then we can take steps to seek amendments to rules that fail to protect our interests. We can try.

Experience really counts and we have become grateful for it as we wade through many frustrations. Not many weeks ago, we found ourselves congratulating one another – and paradoxically thanking Marine Harvest for giving us a rough ride – leading up to the second planning application we were going to have to attend to. The industry gave us the gift of learning at the school of hard knocks and our response was to learn and to cope. Instead of having the steam roller of big business crush us at the outset, we would and could fight. We might lose – because big business usually gets its own way – but we would have fought valiantly, on a foundation of knowledge and experience; as far as we had got, anyway.

The more we study the fish farm issue, the more we know about it and the clearer we can see the appalling harm net-cage fish farms can do and the remedy. We are also now fully aware of the tactics the aquaculture industry thinks we don't see, either because we don't know where to look or because we're just too stupid.

Now we know they are wrong if they think that way, even though in practice they can probably still trample all over us. This book is the result of eighteen months panic and avid learning by people with better things to do, but who care about the place they live. Because a number of us have been learning and working together, it should be considered a collaborative effort, even though it has only one obvious author with a couple of specialist assistants. Indeed, the author's colleagues have all had the opportunity of input, so it is surely a team effort.

However, any optimism the reader may have acquired through reading this chapter must necessarily be short-lived. We have been assured by SNH that the planning process has been designed to favour the developer. We are not at all happy about that (see Chapter 10).

STOP PRESS *On the very day I was preparing this to send for printing we received splendid news. The planners published their decision to refuse the first of the three planning applications for fish farms in the south Skye lochs. When we read the many and diverse refusal criteria, could we detect that the Sleat community's contributions to the public consultation had played their role in informing that decision? Maybe when well briefed, as we are surely becoming, the public really does have a fair say in the planning process. Accumulating enough knowledge and understanding to do the job properly has been (and continues to be) an uphill struggle, but the more we learn about the problem, its solution and the official procedures, the better constructed and more effective the community argument becomes. Thank you for a fair hearing, Highland Council Planning Office. We'll be back – twice – and even better informed.*

Chapter 2

WHAT HAVE THE FISH FARMS EVER DONE FOR US?

The Pros – For Net-Cage Fish Farming

"Over 5 million meals of seafood from Marine Harvest are enjoyed around the world every day. The company offers a wide selection of trusted, sustainable products, sourced from cold clear waters - providing natural, nutritious and delicious seafood." – Marine Harvest[36]

"It was nothing short of fabulous. I had the Loch Duart salmon fillet with the parsnip puree and orange carrot sauce. And it was delightful. What is Loch Duart salmon? I don't know! But I want it AGAIN." – CF, San Francisco[37]

We can take it for granted that the aquaculture industry's executives, management, shareholders and, to a varying degree, depending on status, employees benefit in various ways from salmon farming, or there would be no such industry. This book is not intended to be kind to net-cage aquaculture, as currently conducted, but it seems fair at some stage to consider what we, the public, might stand to gain from the availability of farmed salmon.

1. Cheap salmon, widely available.

"We are proud of the natural environment and pristine waters of Scotland and recognise the vital role our surroundings play in enabling us to produce the finest quality fresh Scottish salmon. Committed to good husbandry ..."
– Scottish Salmon Company[38]

WILD
The Fish Society (wild): Smoked salmon side – wild, Scottish 1020 g **£72.40**
Forman & Field (wild): Genuine Wild Hand-Sliced Smoked Scottish Salmon, Sliced side – 600 g **£59.95**
FARMED
Tesco (farmed): Whole Undressed Salmon Side. 1 kg **£13.00**
FrozenFishDirect.co.uk (farmed): Scottish smoked Salmon 1 kg side **£16.95**

2. Nutritious food.

"Over 5 million meals of seafood from Marine Harvest are enjoyed around the world every day. The company offers a wide selection of trusted,

36 http://www.marineharvest.com/
37 http://www.lochduart.com/
38 http://www.scottishsalmon.com/en/home/homepage

> sustainable[39] products, sourced from cold clear waters[40] – providing natural, nutritious and delicious seafood." – Marine Harvest[41]

Any salmon, *as long as it has excreted any toxins administered and ingested during its upbringing*, ought to be good enough to eat.

3. Employment.

> "The key factor in reaching for our vision "Leading the Blue Revolution" is our 10,400 employees in 22 countries. The company offers a wide range of opportunities worldwide." – Marine Harvest[39]

In spite of optimistic promises, a few new jobs can be offset by local job losses.

> "This proposed fish farm is on traditional creel fishing ground, which I have fished for the past 10 years and will displace us from fishing there, endangering my vessel and our safety. We rely on this area heavily in the winter time where it is more sheltered, but also fish in the summer. This proposed fish farm could make my business economically questionable."
>
> – A Loch Slapin creel fisherman.

4. Economic advantages for communities adjacent to fish farms ...

> "Locally produced salmon helps us attract visitors from all over the world to sample our fantastic seafood menu" – Morefield Hotel, Ullapool

> "Locally produced, high quality salmon ... has kept our business growing" – Ullapool Smokehouse

> "The salmon farming industry is a very important customer for my business, keeping it sustainable[42] and successful" – Ferguson Transport

Those economic advantages can be variously offset by economic disadvantages within the same communities.

> "Visitors from all over the UK, the rest of Europe and Canada are attracted to the area because of the silence, solitude and abundant wildlife, all of which would be adversely affected, should this [fish farm] proposal go ahead. Our business brings both direct employment in support of letting the house and contributes indirectly to the many small businesses, helping to keep people in employment." – A holiday let company, Isle of Skye

5. Gifts of money to local sports teams, schools, pipe bands etc.

> "Sponsorship from salmon farming companies helps keep shinty[43] alive and thriving in the Highlands". – Lochaber Camanchd Club

---

39 Watch out, it's that word again!

40 Where we dispose of our sewage.

41 http://www.marineharvest.com/product/seafood-and-health/

42 That weasel word again. He means "keeping my business sustainable".

43 Shinty (Scottish Gaelic: camanachd, iomain) is a team game played in the Scottish Highlands with sticks and a ball.

"The salmon farming industry has helped us get on the road by supporting our new school minibus." – Ullapool High School

"Ullapool and District Junior Pipe Band has secured a sponsorship deal worth £2,500 from the Scottish Sea Farms Heart of the Community Trust." – Proud to Farm Scottish Salmon

Just one more

"Scottish Sea Farms 'Heart of the Community' Trust – We recognise that success not only depends upon our business competence and investment, but also support from within local communities which allows us to grow and develop.

"The broad aim of the 'Heart of the Community' Trust is to provide financial grants for community projects that deliver lasting change within the regions in which the Company operates." – Scottish Sea Farms[44]

Cynics might wonder whether such donations might be considered not unlike bribery, aimed at gaining loyalty for an unpopular industry, particularly among the young – well, *some* might.

My considered opinion is 

6. "Scottish aquaculture ... provides considerable benefit for fragile economic areas."

I shouldn't need to discuss this because all I need do is slap a copy of *An Assessment of the Benefits to Scotland of Aquaculture* (19 May 2014) on the table and let you read it for yourself. Here's a link to it.[45]

I think we should all attempt to read this report, but I for one just don't 'get' it – at all. I am completely out of synchrony with those who think it's best and good to get out there and harvest as much as we can from the world's resources, not caring about, not even understanding the consequences: running out and wrecking the natural infrastructure that provides those resources. I can't see why making sure a few people have jobs should take precedence over looking after the world we live in. Put the other way round: Why pay people to exploit and damage the natural world just because everybody has to have a job on an overpopulated planet? Who in his or her right mind sees their environment deteriorating, appreciates the reason that's happening and then carries on with business as usual? *Homo sapiens* does.

I just don't think that way, so how can I impartially judge a document like this and not come into conflict with readers who agree with its contents? Unsympathetically and methodically, is how I shall do it.

An Assessment of the Benefits to Scotland of Aquaculture was not written to satisfy anyone concerned about the environmental impact of aquaculture, salmon producing fish farms in particular. The report's approach is made clear in the second of only two

44 http://www.scottishseafarms.com/corporate/heart-of-the-community.html
45 http://www.scotland.gov.uk/Resource/0045/00450799.pdf

paragraphs that constitute the section entitled Research Summary 1:1 Introduction and Methodology:

> "Analysis was split into four work packages:
>
> 1. a macro-level industry assessment;
> 2. a Market Systems Approach analysing the whole market;
> 3. a Sustainable Livelihoods Approach using a combination of interviews and questionnaires to investigate sustainability and benefits to communities; and
> 4. a Value Matrix to summarise all available benefits provided by the aquaculture industry."

Given this four-pronged commercial approach, the curious reader next wishes to know how the researchers obtained their data. Later, in section 4.2, the methodology is 'explained':

> "The methodology undertaken for this assignment was broken down into the four work packages as identified in Figure 5. The macro-level economic analysis was done through desk-based research and clarified through industry interviews both in person and via telephone and email. Value chain and SLA[46] work was conducted through collection of primary data in two work streams – one meeting representatives from throughout value chains and a second undertaking regional and sub-regional interviews and surveys to gather community-level data. All of this information has then been combined using the value chain approach in order to achieve the final value matrix and policy recommendations."

What this means (it's far from clear) is that they asked some people. It seems that the study was mostly based on interviews and questionnaires – *vox pop*. Public opinion can be interesting – to find about opinions – but it is the last thing you want to rely upon to obtain meaningful data. At least two things are wrong with opinion polling:

1. Most people will express an opinion even when they know nothing about the subject; they are very reluctant to say, "I don't know". [The classic case is: "Do you believe in evolution or divine creation?" which is frequently polled. Many people (especially Americans) have been taught they must *believe* in creation whilst very few *know* anything about evolution and are of the opinion (without thinking) that this scientific topic is something you can *choose* to believe or not believe. Their opinion as polled is a matter of dogma and uninformed belief, not factual evidence that may be meaningfully analysed.]

2. Questions asked in even the most objective polls are constructed so that a particular answer gets chosen over another because of preference, not fact. This is very sensibly forbidden in the law courts, the 'leading question', but it is much favoured by pollsters, in particular those who require a predetermined result. [I recall tearing up an airline questionnaire after the first few questions because the answers I would have given were prevented by the way the questions were posed. They wanted me to tell them what they wanted to know, not what was true.]

---

46 Sustainable Livelihoods Approach (see 3. Above).

By whatever means conclusions were reached in *An Assessment of the Benefits to Scotland of Aquaculture*, we can be fairly certain that a lot were based merely upon public opinions, which should be quite unsettling for the properly sceptical[47] reader. Respondents included: fish wholesaler, fish farm employee, restauranteur, hotel manager, fisherman, community council spokesperson etc. whose knowledge is bound to have been partial and/or limited. Many will have had very little knowledge of aquaculture or picked up scraps of popular belief, whilst others will have known plenty about their own sector and little about anything else. Yet all will have expressed their opinions.

Even well informed people can be woefully ignorant on topics that have not impinged upon their thoughtful considerations so far. I should know. Until October 2012 I knew precious little about the subject that was going to occupy me for a long time to come: fish farming. At the same time I thought I knew things that, it turned out, I'd got wrong and even things that were not true. If I examine my knowledge and attitudes honestly I can tell there was little other than vacuity and poorly-considered prejudice present in my mind on the topic of aquaculture. Until then I floundered in a sort of vague confidence that if people are farming fish, then that would be good for the environment because it would reduce pressure on wild fish stocks being over fished. Sheer ignorance! and that was *me* so nobody need take offence at the word (unless they personally identify with the condition and can't take it).

I could not have responded usefully or with honesty to that questionnaire/vox pop study and the same will have applied to a lot of the people who actually took part.

Having got some learning during the past eighteen months, I now know I was seriously wrong and because I understand the subject a lot better, I recognise the fact that I'm not yet certain quite what is right. I have a lot more to learn, but previously I was just plain wrong. If asked any of the questions which form the data set assessed in *An Assessment of the Benefits to Scotland of Aquaculture* I could now answer many with accuracy that would probably surprise the pollsters, accustomed as they will have been with people choosing on a whim which box to tick.

I would also, should the answer not be crystal clear in my mind, reply, with the confidence of one who knows a lot of other things but not this one: "I don't know". I'm glad they had a tick-box for don't know, enabling the respondent to give an honest answer, but which will have made their analysis more complicated ... assuming their vox pop surveys provided them with anything like valid data set. And how does a pollster know when a respondent is ashamed to admit not knowing and makes up an answer?

Please refer to *An Assessment of the Benefits to Scotland of Aquaculture*, but with the large pinch of 'salt' I hope I have competently provided.

---

47 In the sense of always questioning in order to discover the truth.

Chapter 3

NO, WHAT HAVE THE FISH FARMS *REALLY* DONE FOR US?

The Cons – Against Net-Cage Fish Farming

> "EXCEPTIONAL SCOTTISH SALMON The cool, clear waters of the North Atlantic make Scotland the ideal place for raising premium quality salmon and ours is consistently favoured by the most discerning customers, worldwide. It is reared with unrivalled husbandry in an arduous and challenging environment. We are proud it has earned the reputation & respect it deserves as one of the world's tastiest and healthiest foods." – Scottish Sea Farms[48]
>
> "HEALTHY FISH, HEALTHY ENVIRONMENT As farmers, we are guardians of the natural environment. Our sites are monitored on a continual basis for environmental impact, with formal measuring of seabed impact taking place on an annual basis. Local fishermen are even enjoying the benefits of our activity as the areas close to the salmon pens providing ideal sheltered areas for wild fish and shellfish stock enhancement. Hence, when the sites are moved, the fishermen experience good catches.
>
> "We have worked closely with many river owners to enhance the Wild Salmon stocks in local rivers. By providing a year round supply of consistent quality Scottish Salmon, we are reducing the demand for the scarce Wild Salmon where stocks are depleting." – Wester Ross Fisheries Ltd.[49]

Having read these glowing self tributes, can we possibly find fault with salmon farming? Reading the industry's hype leaves you thinking it was a squeaky clean, entirely benevolent practice. "As farmers, we are guardians of the natural environment" indeed?

"Cool, clear waters" may well be "the ideal place for raising premium quality salmon" but what happens to those "cool, clear waters" after fish farms have been installed? (see Chapter 6)

Salmon aquaculture – n.b. as currently conducted – has three monumental defects:

1. Where the fish farms are located.
2. How net-cages are constructed.
3. Reluctance of the industry to invest in environment protection technologies.

Combined, these factors ensure that formerly relatively clean marine ecosystems become dirtied by fish farms and, as a consequence, biodiversity suffers, certainly on the local scale, perhaps – as is surely happening as the number of actively sewage-

---

48 http://www.scottishseafarms.com

49 http://www.wrs.co.uk/environment Ironic: see Chapter 5.

pumping fish farms increases over a prolonged period – through a much greater volume and over wider area of the sea.

Flaws 1 and 2 are unnecessary now that the problems have been identified and solutions devised: containment, which will be discussed later. The industry's stubborn inertia must be dealt with through politics or why should fish farm companies bother to fund costly changes? First the Scottish Government will have to change its policies and apply pressure on behalf of the environment it is so keen to protect.

> "The Convention on Biological Diversity is an international treaty adopted at the Earth Summit in Rio de Janeiro in June 1992. It now has 192 signatories [including the UK]. Scotland as part of the UK has an international obligation to conserve and protect biodiversity."
> – The Scottish Government[50]

> "Alex Salmond's government is failing to live up to many of its ambitious promises on climate change and protecting Scotland's natural heritage, a study [by the Institute for European Environmental Policy] has concluded."
> – *The Guardian*[51]

> "Scotland's seas are home to some truly incredible species and habitats. We want to keep it that way. The life in our seas is fundamentally interconnected by water and the ecosystem processes. Marine protection is meaningless if planning does not account for the fundamental linkages between species and habitats in our seas. Decades of unsustainable activity has resulted in serious damage to areas of Scotland's seas. These areas are now in desperate need of recovery." – Save Scottish Seas[52]

Scotland's seas need a halt to continual assault from unsustainable industrial activities such as net-cage salmon farming.

Fish Farm Location

Salmon aquaculture depends upon clean water, hence the industry's clarion pronouncements, which *always* include 'pristine'[53] to the extent that – like 'sustainable' – I hardly dare use the word these days. In fact when Googling for these quotes, all I had to do was search for various fish farm related terms and company names joined with a + to 'pristine' and they poured in.

> "Scottish salmon is grown in crystal clear, pristine Scottish waters to extremely high specifications meeting stringent animal welfare standards."
> – Salmon Farming in Scotland[54]

50 http://www.scotland.gov.uk/Topics/Environment/Wildlife-Habitats/16118
51 28 October 2013 http://www.theguardian.com/environment/2013/oct/28/scottish-government-failing-climate-wildlife
52 http://www.savescottishseas.org
53 Having its original purity; uncorrupted or unsullied.
54 http://www.saumonecossais.com/en/communication/salmon-farming-in-scotland

> "The Scottish Salmon Company ... credits the pristine Argyll waters and surroundings as the perfect environment for producing the finest quality Scottish salmon." and "The growing army of affluent consumers in the Far East is prepared to pay for high-quality produce from pristine waters, and Scotland is seen to deliver just that." – The Scotsman
>
> "The gourmet selection has been created from salmon farmed in the pristine, wild waters of the Shetland islands." – Hjaltland Seafood
>
> "Our organic salmon thrive in the wild pristine waters along Ireland's westerly coastline." – Marine Harvest
>
> "The Salmon parr are farmed in local freshwater lochs with pristine water quality and high levels of husbandry." – Kames Fish Farming Ltd.
>
> "Scotland has a global reputation as a land synonymous with quality, healthy and highly demanded seafood which is farmed to high standards of best practice, welfare and food hygiene in our pristine Scottish waters."
>
> – Scottish White Fish Producers Association
>
> "Oceanpick began its journey in 2011 with a clear focus on producing top notch marine fish, using the pristine seas for this purpose."
>
> – Colombo Gazette

They like to say that the waters are 'pristine' because that suggests cleanliness of the product, but what they don't mention is that once fish farms have been installed, 'pristine' waters become 'unpristine', if assaulted continuously with aquaculture effluent, maybe forever. But this is speculation – a warning nevertheless – and we must stick to evidence and deduction.

Like the last quote, referring to Sri Lanka, all of these *use* – some might not unjustifiably say *abuse* – the pristine waters of Scottish seas for fish production. The meaning of 'use' might slip unnoticed past the reader, assumed to mean something benign like 'occupy', but in reality it means 'exploit'. Quite how fish farms exploit pristine waters will become apparent as this discussion progresses.

Other requirements are reasonable shelter, so that the fish farm doesn't get demolished by winter storms, plus tides and currents to flush away the fishes' metabolic waste. It's quite difficult to find locations with open water *and* shelter that is cold and clean enough to satisfy salmon, the most fastidious of fishes, but several places around the world supply the aquaculturalists' special needs: Norway, Western Canada, Orkney & Shetland and Western Scotland. What the industry needs is fjords, and they have taken over almost every one of them, all around the world. Fish farm companies have allocated the best waters in these territories to themselves until, to all aquacultural intents and purposes, they are full up. There are not many coastal viewpoints from where double row of ten or twelve salmon cages are not visible.

The Scottish Government has kindly produced a map[55] showing where fish farms are located around the coast of Scotland and the northern isles. We'll be referring to this map again later because it illustrates a possibly important ecological coincidence – not in the sense of an unexpected occurrence, but rather, what looks like it might be a meaningful correlation.

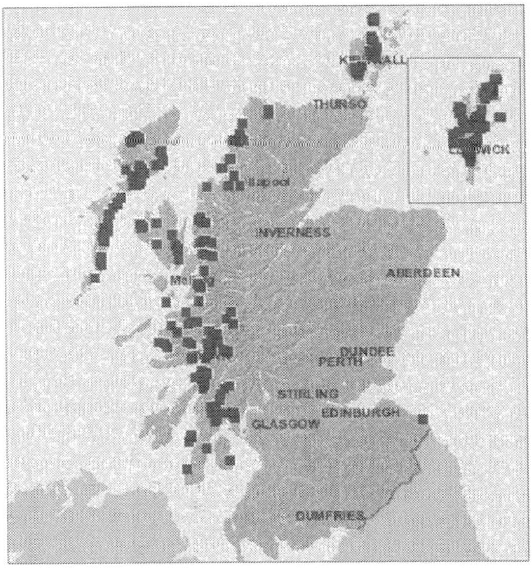

Fish Farm Construction

A modern fish farm, as used in Scotland for salmon culture, consists of ten 120 m circumference (38.2 m diameter) plastic cages[56] and a concrete feed barge (10.5 m x 14 m, 200 tonne capacity).

The sea area occupied by the cages is 150 x 375 m (11459 m^2; 1.14 ha; 2.8 acres; 1½ football pitches) and that occupied by the entire mooring 325 x 560 m (182000 m^2; 18.2 ha; 45 acres; 25½ football pitches).

55 http://aquaculture.scotland.gov.uk/map/map.aspx
56 Previously (as in this picture – Loch Ainort, Isle of Skye) twelve cages 90 m circumference.

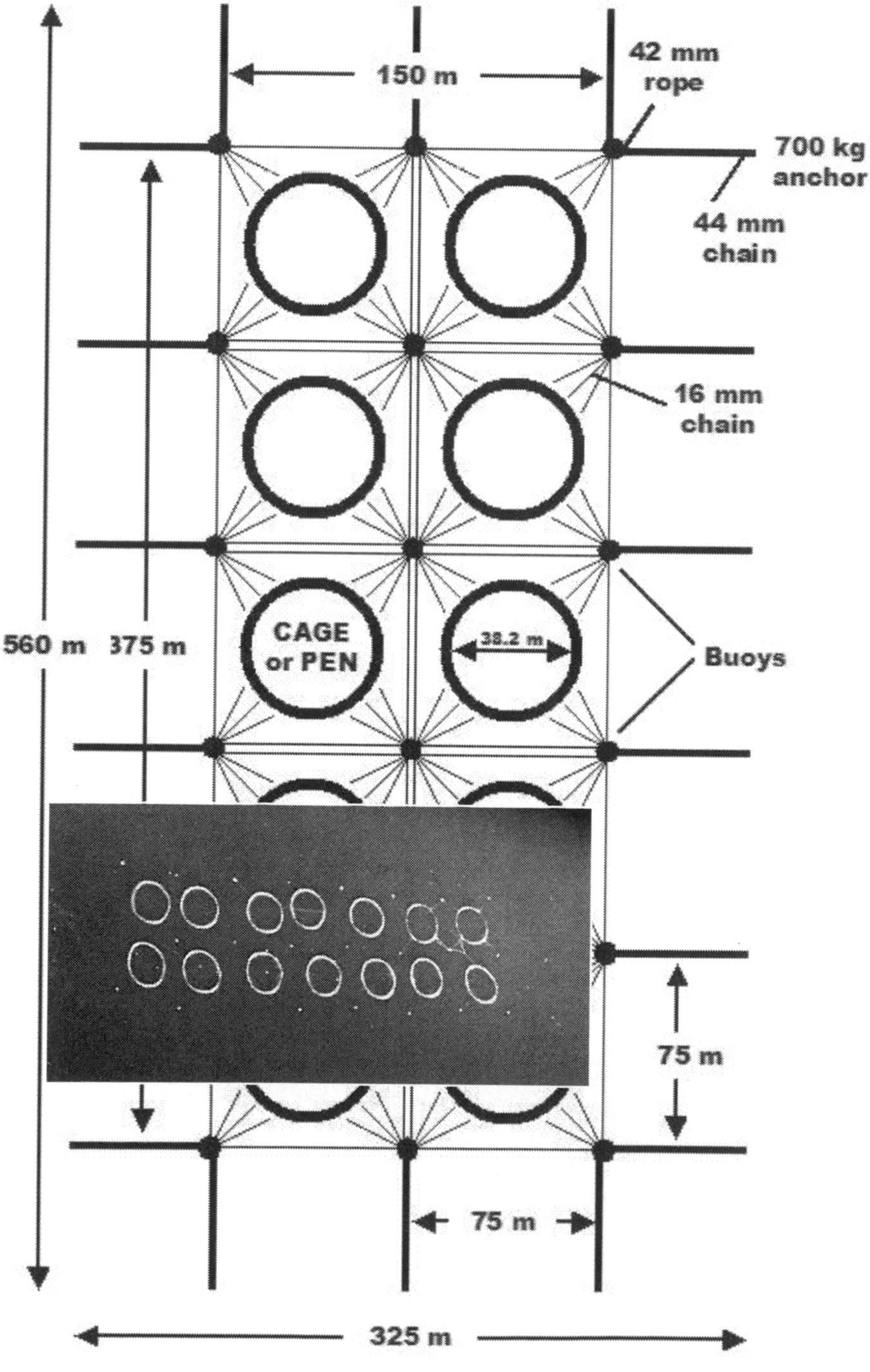

Diagrammatic representation: plan of a modern ten-cage salmon farm. [Inset: aerial photograph showing buoys and some of the moorings.]

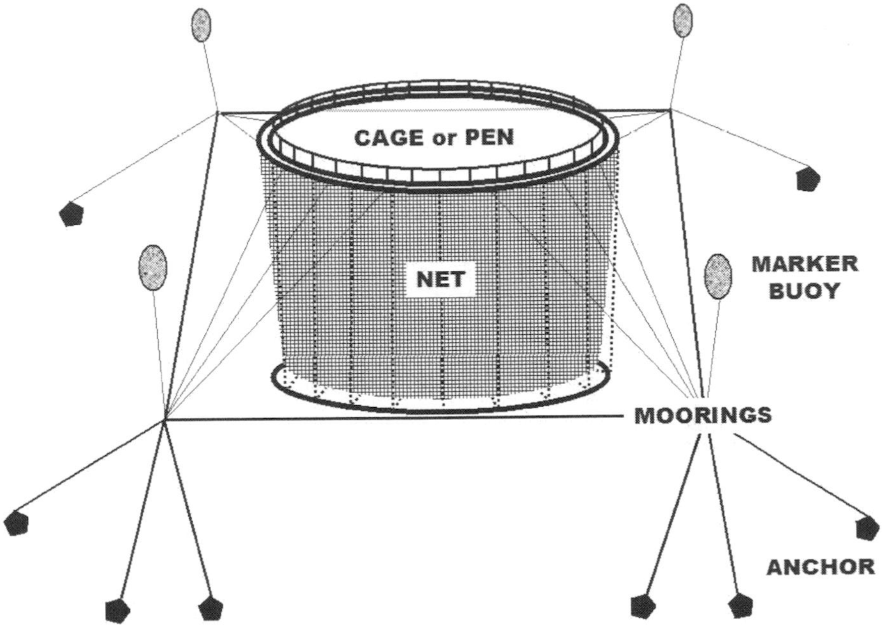

ABOVE: Diagrammatic representation: a single fish farm cage showing the net, guard rail, mooring hawsers, anchors and marker buoys.

BELOW: Two of twelve fish farm pens being serviced. Man on walkway (square) gives an idea of scale.

There is a lot more to the cages or pens than the walkway, top net and feed applicator, visible at the surface. They consist of a broad cylinder of robust plastic netting, held in shape by reinforced circles of tubing and hawsers. They float mostly hidden below the surface.

The turret in the centre of each cage holds a top net aloft, preventing birds swimming or diving into the cage, either eating the fishes or getting trapped. Meanwhile, below, the fishes have room to jump out of the water without getting snagged.

The plastic pipes that link the cages are all connected to the feed barge which holds a stock of feed and sends it, when a computer senses it is needed, to each cage.

In automated feeding systems with a feed barge, the turret is occupied by a rotating curved tube (inset) that delivers feed pellets as required, scattering them onto the water surface.

The Big Trouble With Net-Cages is the HOLES

> Net: a bag or other contrivance of strong thread or cord worked into an open, meshed fabric, for catching (*or containing*) fish, birds, or other animals.
>
> Netting: open-meshed material made by knotting together twine, wire, rope, or thread.

A modern net-cage salmon farm is a splendid example of engineering ingenuity and design. There is nothing much wrong with a modern fish farm ... except the millions of holes of which make up most of a fish farm, holes that let out all the fish faeces and other waste that then becomes a potential (I would say *certain*) pollutant.

Nets are essentially lots of holes tied together with string – complexes of knots with large spaces in between – very loose knitting. Nets are *defined* by their constituent *holes*.

Holes are the cause of all the trouble with fish farms – just about all the trouble. If it weren't for the holes, I doubt the anti-fish farm lobby would exist. Without net-cage holes there would be no mass leakage of fish filth into the sea. If salmon farms were made of something other than holes I would never have gone to the considerable trouble writing this book and making myself unpopular with fish farm people who could, under different circumstances, be my friends.

The thing is that if farmed salmon were fully contained and all their fish muck gathered up for treatment and safe disposal or recycling, there would be nothing for us to complain about (assuming the industry didn't decide to offend our sensitivities in alternative ways).

> "Aquaculture has the potential to impact on the marine environment through the release of solid and dissolved waste, as well as chemical residues.
>
> "Nutrient enrichment from nitrogen waste has been calculated using the nutrient enrichment model developed by the government agency Marine Science Scotland. The level of nutrient enrichment will be small and not sufficient to cause significant impacts on water quality.
>
> "Chemical residues from the fish farm due to sea lice bath treatments have been calculated using the computer model Bath Auto which was developed by the Scottish Environment Protection Agency (SEPA). Impacts from the in-feed sea lice treatment, SLICE, have been calculated using the computer package AutoDepomod. Proposed treatment levels are within SEPA authorised levels. SLICE levels will be monitored to ensure that levels in the sediment do not breach levels permitted by SEPA."
>
> – Hjaltland Seafoods, 2014

I can hear the protests: "We will be monitoring outputs to ensure they do not breach levels permitted by SEPA ..." but that does not mean that there will not still be a constant seepage of effluent into the sea with the potential for accumulation and serious harm to marine organisms and ecosystem functioning. It also does not mean that, in future, SEPA limits will not be exceeded.

> "By far the worst pollution was found in Loch Shell on the east of Lewis near a fish farm operated by the Norwegian-owned company, Marine Harvest [out of 12 Scottish salmon farms]. There, levels of a pesticide called teflubenzuron, were up to 455 times higher than Sepa's environmental quality standards in 2012.
>
> "Of the 19 [fish farms out of 24] with detectable pollution, 12 showed levels of pesticides in breach of SEPA's environmental standards." – *The Herald*[57]

This does not, to my mind, encourage one to confidence that the aquaculture industry has control over its procedures, which would be much improved if everything were to be contained.

That is no more than a hint as to what is going on with regard to levels of pesticide released into the sea in the vicinity of certain (if not all) net-cage salmon farms. The other, perhaps greater worry is the wholesale release of faeces through the holes in the nets into the sea. All – yes, ALL – faeces from all the salmon in every Scottish fish farm goes though the nets, straight into the sea. It might be instructive to calculate just how much that might be.

How many farmed salmon are there in Scotland, pooing into the sea lochs? We can do a back-of-an-envelope calculation to get a reasonable idea.

Firstly, a single cage, depending on its size, can contain between 50,000 and 90,000 salmon.

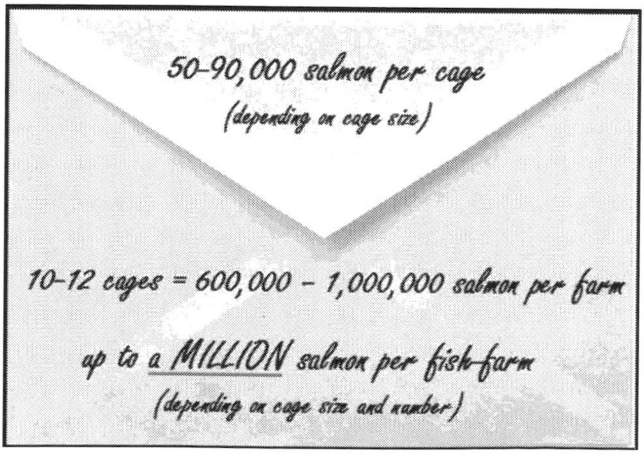

57 Rob Edwards (2013). Pesticides from salmon farms poison Scotland's lochs. The Herald. http://www.heraldscotland.com/news/environment/pesticides-from-salmon-farms-poison-scotlands-lochs.20994497

So there may be up to a million salmon in a single fish farm. Next we need to know how many fish farms there are in Scotland. Scott Landsburgh, spokesman for the Scottish Salmon Producers' Organisation, recently told us during his appearance on *Countryfile*: "Two hundred and fifty seven farms of which about a hundred and fifty seven active at any given time." To err on the conservative side, I've taken the lower estimate for number of fishes per farm, 600,000, and we finish up with a total for farmed salmon in Scotland of around about one hundred million.

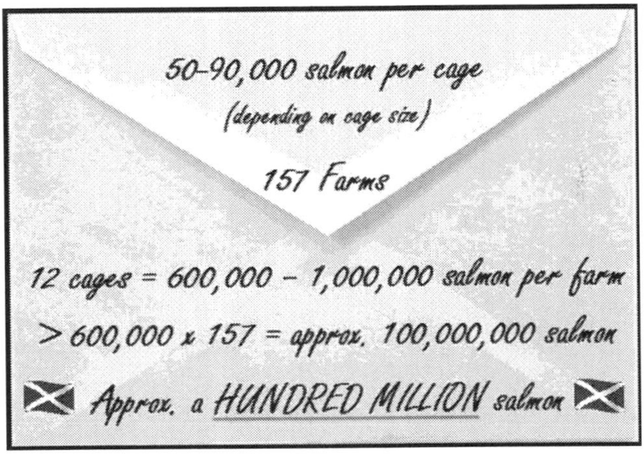

That's one hundred million salmon all dumping in the sea twenty-four/seven. I think we may hazard that that's an awful lot of fish excrement. In fact the independent marine scientist Malcolm MacGarvin calculated back in 2000 (n.b. when fish farms were smaller and fewer) that salmon faecal output was approximately equivalent to the sewage produced by Scotland's human population.[58] That really is awful!

What happens to all that fish sewage after it has sieved through the open sewer that is a fish cage? The fish farms assure us (which version of the story you are told depends who you talk to) that it flushes away harmlessly on the tide, except that negligible quantities (quite how much depends on who you talk to) sink to the bottom where (its fate depends on who you talk to) it gets eaten up by masses of helpful little worms that were there anyway and made safe. Anyway, the fish farms assure us that their fish sewage releases conform to SEPA guidelines, so that's alright.

Actually, I tend to disagree with SEPA, not really something an obedient citizen ought to do(!). After all, they are our representatives, protecting us from malfeasance of commercial concerns. Actually, I find that I often disagree with SEPA, Scottish Natural Heritage and Marine Scotland Science and – I think this might be significant – my 'line manager' is not the Scottish Government, whose publicised ambition is to double salmon exports to the rest of the world. My line manager is a combination of

58 Quoted by *Telegraph* columnist Charles Clover, author of book and film concerned about overfishing The End of the Line. http://www.telegraph.co.uk/news/uknews/1355936/Pollution-from-fish-farms-as-bad-as-sewage.html

my intellect, my expertise as a biologist and my passion for nature. Decisions can vary quite a lot depending on which salary-paying boss is standing behind you.

Why Salmon?

I sat with a friend on a coastal hilltop, looking out across Loch Alsh where two salmon farms adorned the seascape. The occasion was memorable because he introduced me to a new idea, a new thought process in which we considered why salmon should be a favoured farmed fish. It is one of the most difficult because of its lifestyle and life cycle. You can't just bung eggs in a tank and wait for them to grow up to eating size, fed on easily obtained scraps or cheap vegetable matter. Salmon is a top predator that in the wild exclusively eats high quality meat in the form of other fishes, which it chases vigorously. To remain fit and good to eat it needs plenty of exercise or it becomes mushy.

> "[I]t takes about three pounds of wild fish to feed one pound of salmon. So you are likely eating three pounds of jack mackerel or other wild species -- which are likely in trouble -- when you sit down to eat your pound of farmed salmon.
>
> "The answer to this problem is to make salmon aquaculture sustainable. It's to make wild fish stocks more abundant using science-based fishery management instead of promoting salmon farming, which is a destructive and wasteful way of eating wild fish. As long as fisheries are managed properly, wild seafood can provide a healthy meal a day for billions of people.
>
> "Eating three pounds of jack mackerel straight from the oceans to your plate is a far better choice for the environment and for your health. By eating less-popular species you can still enjoy a healthy, wild fish, and our ocean waters can stay free of the pollutants that come with salmon farms. But this won't happen if we keep on grinding our wild fish stocks up to turn them into salmon fish-food." – Ted Danson & Andrew Sharpless[59]

Other fish species have a less demanding appetite, but we either want salmon as well as inferior fish or we can't be bothered with the latter. We demand salmon. If there's a demand, then there's a market and businessmen willing to satisfy that market, as long as they can line their pockets in the process. Fish farming has proved to be a gravy train upon which more and more businessmen want to travel. The more salmon is produced, the cheaper it gets, so demand for farmed salmon keeps increasing as does the need for fish-based salmon feed. Politicians see farmed salmon as a source of revenue, happy voters and success at election time, so they tend to favour fish farming whilst overlooking depredation of wild fish stocks and pollution of the sea.

Meanwhile the fish farm industry is satisfied with the way things are and while we 'environmentalists' keep pointing out that there are flaws in the system, they and their politician pals would prefer no change, the quiet (prosperous) life. We say, "You can't

---

59 Farmed Salmon are Not a Sustainable Alternative. Huffington Post 26 September 2013. http://www.huffingtonpost.com/ted-danson/farmed-salmon_b_3998271.html

just keep dumping all that fish sewage in our seas, especially the clean waters of the Scottish lochs. You have to clean up your act. Upgrade to closed containment." Their response is twofold: 1. Ignore or find ways to justify the sewage problem; 2. Complain that any radical change in methodology would cost them too much money.

Well, I say to them, "Too bad. We would still prefer that you don't use Scotland's lochs as your personal open sewer. You have financial resources. Use them or get out." Oh dear. It's a tough world we live in, where we can't always get everything we want, can't always have our own way.

Is Farmed Salmon so Good to Eat?

> "Salmon is universally acclaimed to be a key part of a healthy diet and Marine Harvest takes great pride in delivering a tasty, nutritious and sustainable product that is enjoyed by five million people around the world everyday.
>
> "The UN Food and Agriculture Organisation reports, 'Fish is a food of excellent nutritional value, providing high quality protein and a wide variety of vitamins and minerals, including vitamins A and D, phosphorus, magnesium, selenium and iodine in marine fish.'
>
> "The presence of these vitamins, minerals and essential fatty acids, makes seafood a healthy choice good for both physical and mental wellbeing and is widely recognised as good nutrition by health authorities, dietary specialists and many others." – Marine Harvest

N.B. The above remarks, although hype from the biggest salmon farming company in the world, cleverly refer to salmon in general and fish in general. Marine Harvest is effectively hijacking wild salmon's good reputation to dress-up an arguably inferior product. Next, an undisguised direct reference to farmed salmon.

> "Farmed salmon, which is what I can afford right now, needs a careful hand if it is not to be pink pap." – Nigel Slater[60]

Those who are privileged to eat wild salmon in all its expressions – steak, fillet, smoked, hot smoked – tell us that conventionally farmed salmon is inferior, lacking its firm texture and, if not artificially dyed, also its colour. Fish farmers who use contained systems employing machinery that creates realistic currents in the water claim that their fishes, obliged to swim energetically, are well exercised and have a firmer flesh.

Because of its artificial diet, farmed salmon can be either pallid grey or all shades of vivid salmon pink, literally dyed[61] through their feed.

---

60 The Observer, Sunday 27 May 2001.
http://www.theguardian.com/lifeandstyle/2001/may/27/foodanddrink.recipes

61 Sometimes using the natural carotenoid astaxanthin but many firms use artificial pink dye.

"Looks mean a lot, and one way that consumers assess the quality of salmon and trout is by the color of the flesh. Our CAROPHYLL® Pink is a proven way to deliver fish that is attractive to the eye."[62]

I won't attempt to judge these pigments. They might be perfectly safe and internet searches tend to find so many far-fetched outrage sites it's difficult to be sure what is true and what is alarmist.

However, like Nigel Slater, chefs who specialise in and know about fish for eating seem to be underwhelmed by farmed salmon. Importantly, they give reasons for the reservations they express.

The Independent "Until recently, only two species of fish, rainbow trout and salmon, have been farmed in quantity. In neither case has the farming been a great success. Farmed rainbow trout is widely regarded as a water-exuding, flaccid travesty of what was once a fine, athletic fish. And despite the wide availability and price advantage of farmed salmon, chefs and food-lovers prefer wild salmon or sea trout.

"Industry experts (and make no mistake, fish farming is an industry) put such reactions down to snobbery and prejudice, and say objective comparisons between wild and farmed fish are rare and generally inconclusive. But earlier this year, the French consumer magazine *Que Choisir* (equivalent to Which?) conducted the largest and most comprehensive analysis and blind tasting to date of farmed and wild fish. The results revealed an ocean of difference between the two types.

"Unfortunately on the day of the tasting there were storms at sea, so no wild salmon was available. How a wild salmon would have compared remains a matter of conjecture; but, according to Mr [Rick] Stein, farmed salmon never matches wild. 'The worst stuff tastes very earthy, the better stuff is rather dull and hard to describe, while wild salmon has a sweet, fresh, nutty quality that you never get in farmed varieties.'

"Environmentalists, too, view the ascendancy of farmed fish as nothing short of disastrous. Ever since salmon farming started in Scottish lochs, there have been complaints about pollution from effluent, the use of colourings to make the fish pink, and the effects of toxic chemicals used to kill the sea lice, which fish kept in cages attract. In 1990, residues of antibiotics and the toxic chemical Dichlorvos were found in samples of fresh salmon on sale, proof that these pollutants find their way into our food." – Joanna Blythman[63]

---

62 DSM in Animal nutrition & health http://www.dsm.com/markets/anh/en_US/products/products-carotenoids/products-carotenoids-carophyll/products-carotenoids-carophyll-fishandshrimp.html

63 The Independent Saturday 30 July 1994 http://www.independent.co.uk/life-style/food-and-drink/sinister-secrets-from-the-lagoon-are-critics-of-fish-farming-just-food-snobs-or-is-aquaculture-bad-for-the-fish-and-its-environment-joanna-blythman-investigates-1417157.html

Slow Fish "Once a luxury food reserved for special occasions like Christmas and New Year's Eve, salmon has gradually become available year-round in supermarkets, in large quantities and at reasonable prices (for the budget of the average Western family). But we should not be deceived by this availability: Salmon is anything but a sustainable fish.

"The stocks of wild Atlantic salmon have been reduced to dangerously low levels. The reasons are many: overfishing, pollution, environmental changes, aquaculture, habitat deterioration and disturbances of migration routes. Wild Atlantic salmon stocks in North America, Europe and the Baltic have been over-exploited since the 19th century and in many regions the species has disappeared completely.

"Even though wild Atlantic salmon stocks have been drastically depleted, farming represents a poor alternative, given the environmental havoc it causes.

"Responding to market demand, in the last ten years aquaculture has increased by over 400%. The majority of salmon are raised in open pens and cages along the coast, where the fish are targeted by predators such as seals and sea birds, who attempt to get through the nets. As a result, many salmon escape from their enclosures. These escapees threaten the wild species, increasing competition for food and for places to spawn and fertilize eggs.

"Fish farms pump uneaten food, a massive amount of excrement and often pesticides and antibiotics directly into the ocean, polluting the water. Farmed salmon suffer from parasites and diseases that can pass to the wild fish, further threatening their populations.

"Additionally, the huge quantity of wild fish needed to feed farmed salmon (it takes between 2.5 and 5 kilos of wild fish to produce 1 kilo of farmed salmon) means that aquaculture consumes more fish than it produces, further increasing pressure on wild species." – Slow Food[64]

If you have never heard of the Slow Food movement, you are unlikely to be impressed by what I have quoted above. So, to clarify:

"Slow Food is a global, grassroots organization with supporters in 150 countries around the world who are linking the pleasure of good food with a commitment to their community and the environment. Slow Food was founded to counter the rise of fast food and fast life, the disappearance of local food traditions and peoples' dwindling interest in the food they eat, where it comes from, how it tastes and how our food choices affect the rest of the world. Slow Food unites the pleasure of food with responsibility, sustainability and harmony with nature." – Carlo Petrini[65]

64 http://www.slowfood.com/slowfish/pagine/eng/pagina.lasso?-id_pg=88
65 Slow Food founder & President http://www.slowfood.com

There's no beating about the bush here. Slow Food's advice is crystal clear and carries a considerable weight of authority:

Not On My Plate
Don't eat wild Atlantic salmon and farmed salmon.[12]

Scottish Salmon? British Aquaculture?

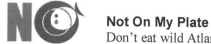

The phrase 'Scottish Salmon' automatically conjures up images in the human mind, romantic images about which the aquaculture industry will be well aware and keen to exploit by doing nothing to disabuse those of us who get taken in. Anyone who is not fully aware of how most supermarket salmon is produced by intensive fish farming will instinctively imagine a tweed-hatted, chest-wadered angler, standing in the sparkling clear waters of a Highland river, twitching his fly across the surface until he eventually lands a magnificent 10-15 kg fish to take home for a traditional Caledonian feast at his castle. That's the image they want you to keep in your mind while you shop for their less natural, but cheaper, alternative.

I have heard it said that much of the salmon we buy in British supermarkets labelled 'Scottish Salmon' has been produced in Norwegian salmon farms, to fill great gaps on the shelves left by real farmed Scottish salmon, which has mostly been exported to China, India etc. I don't know if that's true – you can check it on the internet for yourself, though be careful (of course) not to be taken in by incompetent, biased and downright dishonest websites.

What I do know about aquaculture companies, because I've checked them, is that the majority[66] of salmon farming companies are not Scottish, not even British, but Norwegian (with a little Swiss interest). You don't need me to list them, because you can quickly find out for yourself: Marine Harvest, Hjaltland, Scottish Sea Farms, Scottish Salmon Company, Meridian Salmon Group are the major companies and none of them is British. Unless I've missed something (apologies for being suspicious) ... unless I'm mistaken, the small companies are the only Scottish owned: e.g. Kames, Wester Ross Fisheries, Loch Duart. Apart from fish farm companies' own websites, *Company Check*[67] makes an interesting excursion (just for contextual information, you understand).

Does it matter that 'Scottish Salmon' is manufactured and sold by Norwegians? Does it matter if 'Scottish Salmon' might actually be Norwegian fish? I really don't know, but we need to be aware of any such anomalies, about which – being someone who is rather firmly attached to the truth – I feel rather uneasy. I suspect that fish purchasers are not being fully informed so that they might remain uncertain who's who and what's what, even if they care to inquire.

Why should that be so?

---

66 In this case it would be legitimate to use the now horribly clichéd 'vast majority', which these days can mean any majority in excess of 50%. By majority, I really mean majority.
67 http://companycheck.co.uk

Chapter 4

PUBLIC OBJECTIONS TO NET-CAGE FISH FARMING

"Dear Sir or Madam, I wish to object to the above planning application on the following grounds, in summary: 1. BIODIVERSITY This development would pose a threat to a range of Biodiversity Action Plan habitats. It would also threaten a wide range of associated wildlife, including several specially protected species. 2. LANDSCAPE This development would have a negative impact on an iconic landscape and also the adjacent National Scenic Area 3. POLLUTION Effluent associated with fish faeces and waste food would pose a pollution risk. 4. DISEASE Fish lice associated with farmed salmon would pose a risk to wild salmon and sea trout populations. 5. ECONOMIC IMPACT The negative economic impact of this development, especially concerning tourism and also other fisheries interests, far outweigh employment gains through the development."

– Concise public consultation letter objecting to a proposed fish farm

Each fish farm planning application is submitted to the local council accompanied by a suite of documents prepared by the applicant and also by various advisory bodies: Scottish Natural Heritage, the Scottish Environment Protection Agency, Marine Scotland, Historic Scotland, The Crown Estates, the council's Historic Environment Team and Policy and Information officer, Transport Scotland and the local wild fisheries board(s). Once all of those documents have been received by the planning office and uploaded to their website a public consultation is opened, usually of about one month's duration. It is then that we, the public, may comment for or against.

People have very varied points of view and tend to emphasise what matters to them most. What follows divides people's objections into ten categories, eight in this chapter under sub-headings and then two to follow as separate chapters (5 & 6), the biological arguments which cause me to write the longest letters (and a book) and give me more sleepless nights than the others.

Visual Impacts - Everybody

The Scottish sea lochs and their surroundings comprise some of the most peaceful and beautiful scenery to be found anywhere in Britain with few distractions from the natural to offend the eye, ear or mind. Maybe they should be considered places requiring jealous conservation, not industrial development. This is a big consideration but requires few words because we all know what we think about the visual intrusiveness or otherwise of fish farms in the landscape.

Other Detrimental Impacts – Tourism

On Skye, visitors flock to the loch shores to sit and stare – the views are marvellous – or indulge in more strenuous activities: walking, climbing, exploring, nature study etc. There is a network of popular walks to attract British and foreign individuals and parties, often in significant numbers (e.g. 25 counted along the Borreraig-Suisnish trail on one occasion was not exceptional). Do fish farms improve the landscape/seascape and what do visitors think of their presence? Are they inconspicuous and are they passed by, unnoticed? Does the constant rumble of their generators and feed barge engines spoil peacefulness of loch shores, annoying locals within earshot and deterring visitors? Will fish farms in the lochs blight the fabulous views that energetic climbers may enjoy from the mountain tops?

Obstruction of Local Fishing Grounds

The site chosen by aquaculture companies for their fish farms often have a sea bed consisting of a JNCC[68] determined Priority Habitat known as burrowed mud with sea pens and other macrofauna [SS.SMu.CFiMu.SpnMeg] which is considered by SNH to be a Priority Marine Feature (PMF).

The 'other macrofauna' usually includes significant numbers of *Nephrops norvegicus* (Langoustine, Norway Lobster, Dublin Bay Prawn, Scampi), the 'Prawns' much relied upon by West Highland creel fishermen for their living.

A sample Environmental[69] Statement from a fish farm planning application claims: "The site will remove a small area of potentially suitable fishing ground and it is likely that directly beneath the cages, in the area 'degraded' due to organic enrichment, that Nephrops will be excluded."

Firstly, hard evidence from other fish-farm sites shows that the word degraded in the above quotation has been inappropriately placed between inverted commas. It is not an ironic term (as 'degraded' implies), but literally true. The sea bed (and more besides) *will* become degraded by organic enrichment caused by sewage outfall from a fish farm and that any *Nephrops* living there will be *exterminated.*

Second, creel fishermen take a different view of the potential loss of fishing ground, which they consider would be not inconsiderable. Of the few features discernible in Hjaltland's underwater camera video footage, one is striking: the density of burrow openings on the sea floor, which might well have been constructed by a thriving population of *Nephrops*.

> "We rely on this area heavily in the winter time where it is more sheltered, but also fish in the summer. This proposed fish farm could make my business economically questionable. I am a young local person with a young family and depend on fishing to support them." – Skye creel fisherman

---

68 Joint Nature Conservation Committee http://jncc.defra.gov.uk/

69 The pedant in me is irritated by the use of the adjective 'environmental' in this sort of context, but that's what it's called. It's not the statement that's environmental. It should be called an Environment Statement or something else.

Equivocal Benefit-Detriment for Employment Prospects

> "They had claimed that the environmental standards were absurdly strict and were costing the regions jobs and hurting the economy (the polluters' favorite mantra)." – Donald Prothero[70]

All fish-farm applications and publicity come laced with extravagant claims for employment prospects; that the fish farm will mean more jobs for the local unemployed. Such claims generally exceed reality and fail to account for concomitant employment losses, such as:

1. Restrictions to the viability of creel fisheries;
2. Pollution impacts (direct and algal blooms) on shellfish cultivation;
3. Impacts on accommodation providers at adjacent popular tourism hotspots;
4. Reductions in a variety of local tourist dependent incomes if tourists are deterred.

> "I am opposed to the salmon farm proposal for the following reasons: As a former salmon farm, site supervisor, I have observed the gradual decline in the numbers employed per site as mechanisation improvements are made. The promise of numbers of staff employed is likely to continue to decrease with time." – Objection comment in fish farm consultation

Promises of Local Economy Enhancement

> Using Scottish Government wage multipliers, this [wage bill, for 8 full time staff, of approximately £200,000] gives an approximate value of £540,000 to the local economy. – Fish Farm Promise

This promise was inflated to account for three fish-farms in the south Skye loch system and was over optimistic, failing to allow for potential losses that might simultaneously be experienced by the local economy.

Local accommodation providers who rely on tourism for their income feel that fish farms in the view from their property will discourage regular visitors from returning. Objection letters sent in by regular Skye visitors to public consultations confirm this concern.

Industry PR reckons that increased local employment will benefit local businesses such as shops. Apart from the fact that most people have to travel away from the area for shopping, as discussed earlier, employment enhancement is likely to be offset by loss of work in other trades (such as fishing). These sorts of PR promises by fish farm representatives don't seem to hold a lot of water.

Apparently generous gifts to community organisations should surely be met with circumspection? They might well be considered to be cynical bribes intended to gain approval for and even loyalty to an industry that is not universally popular.

---

70 Prothero, Donald R. (2013). Reality Check: How Science Deniers Threaten Our Future. Indiana University Press.

Sensitive Wildlife

> "Conserving Scotland's marine environment is not just desirable – it is essential to ensure our seas remain healthy and productive into the future."
> – MS, SNH & JNCC[71]

Scottish sea lochs contain some of the best marine biodiversity in the country. Divers see a lot of this while land-locked biologists get a very good idea by examining the ecology of the seashore. That's my particular forte. In response to fish farm planning applications and the need for data to inform SNH during their deliberations prior to the 2014 designation of Marine Protected Areas I produced a spreadsheet recording all the special and rare species local biologists have found on the shores of Lochs Slapin and Eishort.

The outcome was startling, finding a total of twenty-six previously unrecorded creatures, including several hardly ever (one never) found in the Highlands until now.

Effluent from net-cage salmon farms is a significant pollution hazard that could affect any of these potentially sensitive species and several important habitats. In my opinion – which accords with the Precautionary Principle devised at the United Nations' 1992 Rio World Summit – before any development (or pollution) begins, we have to find out what will happen to animals and plants in the sea and on the shore.

> The Precautionary Principle – "Principle 15. In order to protect the environment, the precautionary approach shall be widely applied by States according to their capabilities. Where there are threats of serious or irreversible damage, lack of full scientific certainty shall not be used as a reason for postponing cost-effective measures to prevent environmental degradation." – Rio Declaration, 1992[72]

Read more about this in Chapter 6.

Wild Animals Interact with Fish Farms

Many people show concern about predatory animals, not without good cause. Apart from marine invertebrates, quite a few other animals live in the vicinity of Scottish loch installed fish farms and many of them like to eat salmon. Having no conscience they find a cage full of fishes impossible to resist.

A government publication by the Fisheries Research Services surveyed reports of predator attack on fish farms in Scotland.[73]

> "Throughout Scotland, managers of the 195 sites surveyed reported 12 species of predator to cause problems at farms. Seals (both grey and harbour) were the most common predators, being reported at 81% of sites. There was significant regional variation in the numbers of farms that suffered loss or

71 Large poster produced jointly by Marine Scotland, Scottish Natural Heritage and the Joint Nature Conservation Committee seen in the entrance to SNH headquarters, Inverness.

72 http://www.unep.org/Documents.Multilingual/Default.asp?DocumentID=78&ArticleID=1163

73 Predators at Scottish Salmon Farms http://www.scotland.gov.uk/Uploads/Documents/FW04Predators.pdf

damage due to seals, otters, mink and herons, but not from the other species of predator."

Harbour seal < 140
Grey Seal < 120
Shag > 80
Heron < 80
Cormorant < 80
Gull ~ 50
Otter ~ 35
Mink 20
Gannet ~ 5
Fulmar ~ 4

The most controversial attackers of farmed salmon are indeed harbour (common) seal *Phoca vitulina* and grey seal *Halichoerus grypus*, which will exploit any weakness they find in a fish cage and will wreak havoc that fish farmers do not tolerate. They are uncompromising in the steps they take to deter attacks from predatory animals:

> Predators will be excluded by the use of a cage net tensioning system. Top nets will be used to exclude avian predators ... and will be kept fully tensioned by a top net support no more than 2.5 m high to prevent entanglement. Seals are primarily deterred from accessing the stock using tensioning nets of the cages themselves.
>
> If this system were to become insufficient then Hjaltland Seafarms Ltd. would deploy a selectively acoustic deterrent service, an AceAquatec Seal Scrammer. In the event of a seal attack this device detects the panic reaction of fish stock, which then triggers an acoustic release that disturbs the seals and forces them to leave the cage area. This would only be installed if a seal attack occurred and would not emit a continuous acoustic noise.
>
> If however all options of predator deterrent failed, and persistent and highly damaging seal activity occurred, Hjaltland Seafarms Ltd. would like to consider the option of lethal control on no more than **ONE** seal per year. This would require an application to Marine Scotland for a licence and would have to be undertaken by a trained marksman. Any lethal removal of a seal predator would have to be reported to Marine Scotland and would only be undertaken if all over [*sic*] methods had failed to protect the stock and to prevent net damage, potentially leading to escapes.
>
> – from a Hjaltland Seafarms Environmental Statement

Seal Scrammers or Acoustic Deterrent Devices (ADDs) may deter seals, but also "can cause stress, hearing damage and deter non-target species such as dolphins and porpoises from their natural habitat."[74] When the public becomes aware of this it adds greatly to concern about and objection to fish farms.

74 The Scottish Government http://www.scotland.gov.uk/Publications/2013/11/9261/1

Hjaltland promise they will shoot "... no more than **ONE** seal per year", and under licence with a marksman. If all active Scottish salmon farms[75] killed just one seal per year, that would account for the "lethal control" of 157 harbour and grey seals.

Figures for actual numbers of seals shot to protect fish farm stock are difficult to pin down, but none that I can find is anywhere near as 'low' as 157 and reliable hearsay suggests that the higher numbers are the more likely. (Hearsay from similar reasonably trustworthy sources also suggests that killing – often euphemistically referred to as culling – is not always carried out under licence or by a marksman; but that's just hearsay.)

Here are a few estimates:

> Fish farmers in Scotland killing estimated 2,000 seals a year. – Emily Shelton[76]
>
> An estimated 3,500 seals are killed around Scottish fish farms each year as part of 'predator control'. – Philip Lymbury[77]
>
> THE SHETLAND salmon industry has admitted shooting more than 140 seals during the first two years of the Scottish government's latest licensing legislation. – Pete Bevington[78]
>
> According to official figures,[79] fish farmers shot 449 seals in 2011 and 2012 in order to try and prevent them from eating salmon. – Rob Edwards[80]

Birds may try to get at salmon in fish farm cages. Are they deterred by the nets placed to keep them out? Let's hope they never get entangled – net tension is supposed to prevent that. Imagine a gannet diving from 100 ft. Would it just bounce off and fly away unharmed.

Another large predator that feeds on fish and could easily down a salmon is the otter *Lutra lutra*. Rather than discuss its role in fish farm attack I would like us to consider a problem that is becoming recognised in badgers and might be applicable to otters that inevitably live close to Scottish salmon farms.

It seems that badgers are sensitive to – perhaps harmed by – low frequency infra-sound emitted by wind farm generators. Stress hormone levels are elevated in badgers living close to 'windmills'. It is possible that otters with holts situated on the shore adjacent to (2 km) fish farms, which can constantly emit low frequency noise, might suffer similarly. We can say no more now, but be aware that more information requiring serious attention might be forthcoming soon.

---

75 "Two hundred and fifty seven farms of which about a hundred and fifty seven active at any given time." Scott Landsburgh (Scottish Salmon Producers Organisation) interviewed on Countryfile, BBC1, 1 Dec. 2013.

76 Ecologist, 28 September 2010. http://www.theecologist.org/News/news_round_up/613019/fish_farmers_in_scotland_killing_estimated_2000_seals_a_year.html

77 *Compassion in World Farming Trust*, 2002. http://www.ciwf.org.uk/media/3818689/in-too-deep-summary.pdf

78 *Shetland News* 8 May 2013 http://www.shetnews.co.uk/news/6751-almost-150-seals-shot-under-licence

79 The Scottish Government http://www.scotland.gov.uk/Topics/marine/Licensing/SealLicensing

80 http://www.robedwards.com/fish_farming/

The Poor Quality of Planning Applicants' Data and Documents

> "I've been doing some comparisons between the two applications....and quite frankly I have never seen such 'balderdash'." – Anon. (pers. comm.)

Having now encountered several fish farm planning applications I can state with confidence that the standard of documents submitted is appalling. Of course, I haven't seen them all, so some companies might put in competent sets, but recent efforts have been not much better than my school homework when I was an indolent schoolboy. It seems that fish farm companies employ staff who either have little ability or motivation or are willing to sell their souls for the company, and will put in as little work as they possibly can and fudge reports that will scrape through the planning process. The various authorities are so weary of the relentless battering they get from fish farm applications, that now they pretty well just wave them through unchallenged.

I have learnt from gleeful experience that the regulatory authorities are a lot less critical than I am, particularly since I've realised just how easy it is to tear these fish farm documents to shreds; just as my school masters must have done when they worked late at night, marking my slapdash essays (of which, these days, I am embarrassedly ashamed).

Here is what I wrote to the Highland Council's planning office about a fish farm application in 2014:

Careful attention to the documents submitted along with this planning application discovers a number of careless errors, slack attention to proof reading and less than competent use of conventional biological terminology. While these shortcomings do not in themselves constitute grounds for rejection, there are certain deficiencies that lead to the conclusion that the authors either do not care about the outcome of this application or are not sufficiently competent to present it.

<u>IN THE FORMER CASE</u> we have the village name Heaste spelt 'Haste', lens spelt 'lense', sighting spelt 'siting' and *rationale* spelt 'rational'. Even the name of the loch in question has been misspelt in at least one instance ('Slappin') and *Nephrops*[81] burrows is routinely printed (i.e. not a typographical error) as 'Nephrop burrows' in the three ROV data tables. Common names of animals are used throughout these poorly constructed tables, which are too imprecise to facilitate a properly considered appraisal of the operator's findings. Quantification, as presented in these tables in a parody of the conventional ACFORN[82] estimation method, is so vague as to be meaningless. Apart from general misspellings, these and numerous other errors indicate bad scientific practice, thoroughly inappropriate in what purports to be (and should be in this context) a scientific study.

Poor sentence construction leads to difficulties of understanding, for instance what does this mean: "Conclusions. Through careful site selection, management and following best practice the potential impacts on the environment will be minimised as can be reasonably foreseen."?

---

81 From the Greek: Nephron or Nephros (kidney) + Ops (eye). The eyes of *Nephrops norvegicus* are kidney-shaped.

82 Abundant, Common, Frequent, Occasional, Rare, None – which also requires a quantification key, not attempted by this applicant.

IN THE LATTER CASE it is the given location of the proposed fish-farm that gives grave cause for concern about the competence of the authors.

1. Location and Visual Impact Assessment (LVIA) seems to have been submitted three times. Certainly version 2 is different from version 1, whilst version 3 seems to be the same as version 2 with the same title as version 1. The obvious difference is the quality of the simulation photographs, which were very slapdash in version 1, neither resembling the fish-farm as it would be nor sized or positioned convincingly. The improved versions were most welcome, but they seem also to be less accurate than might be hoped for (SNH, pers. comm.)

It is recommended that a third (fourth?) version be requested, in which the proposed fish-farm is depicted in the geographical position intended, at the correct distance from the shore and accurately to scale.

2. The location of the proposed fish-farm seems to have changed several times, though even in the version 2 photomontage, it *seems* to be substantially farther north than it should be. However, the apparent error might be forgiven if the appearance of its too northerly location has been caused by perspective, the photo having been taken a short distance south of the stream in order to record a passer-by's view unobscured by the elevation in the land east of the fish-farm.

3. Application The application form was submitted twice, the amended version providing new location co-ordinates, showing that the originals were inaccurate by approximately 100 m. In itself this might be trivial or even a change to the applicant's plan, but the site is given as 1 km NW of the Cave. Depending on which co-ordinates you take as definitive, this puts the fish-farm 225 m or even 325 m adrift (depending on which of the other two locations are considered), a not inconsiderable discrepancy that does not inspire confidence.

4. Why did the applicant not prepare a Water Quality Report (question 12)? If not required, why is this question in the application at all?

5. Why did the applicant omit to answer question 14 in their first application [Pre-Application Discussion] and then why in the second was 'no' checked. Did they not need to contact the planning authority before submitting their application? If not, why is this question in the application at all?

6. LVIA Comments 1-5 above might seem to be (relatively) trivial. The following, however, appears to be a more serious shortcoming. Checking the figures in Table 1 – Results of the Noise Assessment in all versions of the LVIA showed that the distances from various distant landmarks to the proposed fish-farm are more-or-less accurate. However, two figures stand out among the rest as exaggerated, one by a factor of x2 and the other almost x3. These are the figures for distance between the fish-farm and the two *nearest* landmarks.

One acknowledges that precisely what those nearby landmarks might be has not been made clear (it should be), though one assumes that the 'track' must be the rough road from the north and the 'path' the footpath that comes over the hill. But that might not be the case, because the photograph named according to one of those nearby landmarks has the other in the foreground.

Perhaps it need not concern us exactly which is which, because the two landmarks are close at the photo point. However, the distance given for fish-farm to landmark #1 is 1630 m whereas the actual distance is significantly less than 1,000 m. The distance given for fish-farm to landmark #2 is 2060 m whereas the actual distance cannot be much more than 1,000 m if that.

Why are the distances for the two sites nearest to land, where people most likely to be inconvenienced by noise from the fish-farm, the only inaccurate (exaggerated) ones and why are the discrepancies so marked?

7. ROV[83] REPORT The plan was to drive the ROV along three linear trajectories (transects)[84], one following the long axis of the fish farm site and two across it, filming as it travelled (below, left). It was intended that analysis of the video footage at stations along the three transects would provide meaningful information about the topography and ecology of the sea bed. Demonstrably, the transects missed their intended trajectories (below, right) and the camera footage was simply awful, yet the videos and a cobbled together report were submitted to support the planning application.

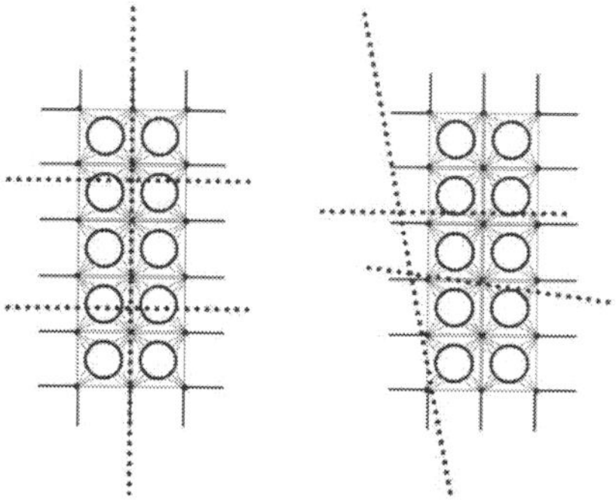

The diagrams provided in the ROV reports showing proposed and actual transect locations, as other defects in this application, fail to inspire confidence that this biological survey was competently conducted. Surely if the weather was so unsuitable on the day that the operators' boat drifted so far off course that the longitudinal transect almost entirely missed the fish-farm site, the process should have been abandoned or repeated as soon as the inaccuracy had been realised? Because of this the ROV data must be considered of limited use and the applicant should be obliged to return to the site and repeat the exercise. These considerations lead one to speculate wryly that, unlike the rest of us, the applicant's employees do not have access to GPS technology.

8. The ROV video footage has been studied. It is evident from observing the behaviour of the ROV that:

a. It did not arrive at the seabed before filming began.
b. It spent much of its time looking upwards or from too great a height (shows blue rather than brown) or occasionally examining its own superstructure.

83 Remotely Operated Vehicle with underwater camera.
84 Transect: a line along which along which observations are made or measurements taken.

c. When it was actually filming the sea bed it undulated wildly, in such a way as to make the viewer feel quite seasick.
d. It often travelled so rapidly that the viewer is unable to keep up and make observations.
e. The compass – screen centre – and the film itself (on the rare occasions when the seabed was visible) showed it spent much of its time revolving, indeed spinning, sometimes well in excess of 360°, rather than following the straight line which defines a transect.
f. It frequently crashed into the sea bed, generating dense clouds of sediment that totally obscured the scene for minutes at a time.
g. When the sea bed could be inspected, for much of the time any biological entities that came into view were indistinct or out of focus, or flashed by too rapidly.

It will be obvious to anyone who views the applicant's ROV footage that it does not constitute a useful or even competent biological study, the primary purpose of the exercise. One wonders why it was not repeated when weather and experience might enable the gathering of meaningful data, and why such appalling material was ever submitted in the first place.

N.B. During the earlier scoping process, SNH stated: "It is important that the techniques used [for a benthic visual survey] provide footage of sufficient quality to identify species observed on the transects."

Because the ROV spent so much of its time not looking at the seabed and on occasions when it did resolution was very poor, this requirement was not met.

In each video clip the co-ordinates showing the location of the travelling ROV (latitude-longitude, degrees-minutes) are provided along the top line of data, albeit with the first figure annoyingly obscured by another label. Therefore, it has been possible to plot the start, middle and end of each ROV transect onto a map (below, left) with the fish-farm site superimposed (below, centre). It can be seen that the three transects shown in the applicant's report, the actual survey transect locations, which we already know missed their intended trajectories, at best describe *idealised* routes for the transects actually travelled. The three straight lines showing 'actual' transects have been drawn in by the applicant joining the end points of each transect and do not show the tortuous route the ROV actually followed (demonstrated below, right).

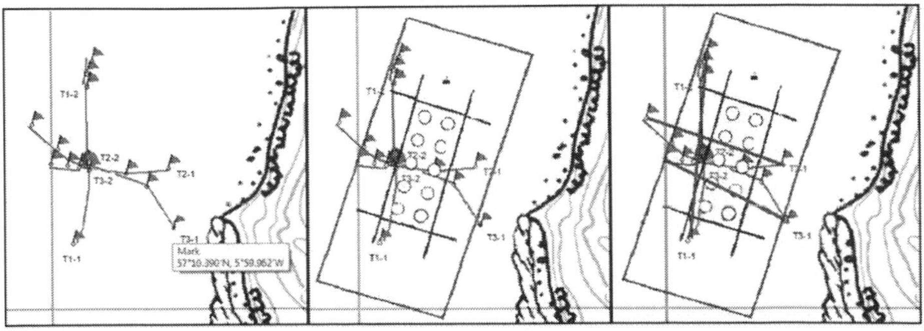

It seems not unreasonable to conclude that the three transects shown in the applicant's report do not depict accurately the actual trajectories of the ROV transects. The judgement whether this is because of skill deficit (amply illustrated by the quality of the ROV video footage) or mendacity is left to the planning officer.

N.B. During the scoping process, SNH stated: "The location of transects should be agreed in discussion with SEPA marine science staff."

Agreed? Perhaps. Achieved? Demonstrably no.

9. Because the ROV video footage is so poor, the applicant's staff have been unable to gather much information from it. Of the 36 still frames provided, many do not depict biological entities, whilst those that do are mostly quite unhelpful (indistinct or out of focus).

Problems of actually seeing anything on the seabed from the ROV camera are highlighted by the paucity of information in the tables describing the three so-called transects. Only nineteen stations have been described for the biological characterisation of the entire 1.14 hectare site, woefully inadequate in a supposed scientific study.

During the brief periods when the camera actually looked at the sea bed it is clear that there is a significant concentration of burrows probably inhabited by *Nephrops norvegicus* (the major fishery in the south Skye lochs). It should be noted (the applicant did not) that some of the larger volcano-like structures on the sea bed sediment might have been made by the rare mud volcano worm *Maxmuelleria lankesteri*, which even a competent surface view might well overlook. This should be investigated.

Data provided in Tables 1-3 (one per transect) are scant and couched mostly in non-biological terms, one of them repeatedly misspelt (eighteen times): Nephrop [*sic*] burrows. The quantification method is hopeless. These might seem to be trivial criticisms, but they reveal that the compiler of this necessarily biological report lacks a grasp of basic biological language and discipline. These deficiencies have been noted throughout the biological reports, such as the Environmental Statement in which similar spelling errors (that are not just typographical, (e.g. *Peachia cylindrical* [*sic*]) occur and standard scientific conventions are either flouted (umol-l) or misused ($\mu moll^{-1}$).

Information provided by the ROV transect report is of a very poor, thoroughly unacceptable standard. Incorrect use of conventional scientific terminology and method ensures that the informed reader can find little that engenders confidence in these reports.

This illustration should be sufficient to show the reader just how poor a fish farm planning application can be. It is not unique. Others from the same company and others have been found, on nit-picking scrutiny, to be equally badly presented; indeed it is quite obvious that reports of ROV and hydrographic surveys have been copied, pasted and then badly edited from previous applications. In one case, old data were found unchanged from a previous application!

Also, a previous submission from a rival fish farm company (the same site) was found, on elementary critical examination, to be equally inept if not worse. One wonders how many times this lazy technique has been used. No schoolboy or undergraduate would get away with such sloppy work, so why should these professionals?

I find it quite insulting to the public and the planners that commercial operators should have so little regard for their intellect. The trouble is that few people ever get to look at, let alone analyse, such documents as they shuttle through the system, unhindered by weary planning officers and their advisers. Meanwhile, industry easily gets away time and again with its accustomed (cheap) shoddiness. We, the public, must grasp the opportunity we surely have available to us to download these planning documents from the internet (see Chapter 10), where they are always completely accessible for our lawful use, and inform the authorities without equivocation of all the deficiencies they contain.

I encourage readers, when commenting on applications, to look critically at any application support documents they feel competent to judge and if they find irregularities such as I have illustrated above, to expose them mercilessly. It's only fair.

Fraud?

I think we need to take the argument about document quality a step further: Surely this careless approach to the planning process constitutes some sort of deception, perhaps outright fraud? I certainly feel as though I am being swindled when fish farms 'supported' by such poor paperwork are approved almost without question. When a local council has rules to prevent installations springing up wherever people want to put them, we are all (I thought) obliged to adhere to those rules. We have to navigate the planning process to the letter if we want permission build a house or even erect a shed, simple porch or decking. If we do it wrong, there are checks in the system that bring us back on track with no arguing. Why should the rules for a large industrial concern be more lenient or flexible than those for a householder with a small project? Why do the planners not take a brief critical glance through these truly substandard fish farm applications and if they do not pass muster, send them back for revision, with no arguing? If plans I have submitted in the past for simple projects had not been of at least reasonable intelligent standard that would have applied to me (actually, I think it did, once).

I know the answer, at least as vouchsafed to me quietly by one of our regulatory inspectors: the Scottish Government, bent on massively increasing salmon production for export, has decreed that salmon farm applications should be favoured.

There are two more major objections that people raise with regard to fish farms. To complete the Chapter 4 list, I will give their headings here, but then devote a separate chapter to each.

The Health of Farmed and Wild Fishes (Chapter 5)

Marine Pollution (Chapter 6)

Chapter 5

THE HEALTH OF FARMED AND WILD FISHES

"The scariest thing is that nobody seems to be considering the impact on those wild fish of fish farming on the scale that is now being proposed on the coast of Norway or in the open ocean off the United States. Fish farming, even with conventional techniques, changes fish within a few generations from an animal like a wild buffalo or a wildebeest to the equivalent of a domestic cow.

"Domesticated salmon, after several generations, are fat, listless things that are good at putting on weight, not swimming up fast-moving rivers. When they get into a river and breed with wild fish, they can damage the wild fish's prospects of surviving to reproduce. When domesticated fish breed with wild fish, studies indicate the breeding success initially goes up, then slumps as the genetically different offspring are far less successful at returning to the river. Many of the salmon in Norwegian rivers, which used to have fine runs of unusually large fish, are now of farmed origin. Domesticated salmon are also prone to potentially lethal diseases, such as infectious salmon anemia, which has meant many thousands have had to be quarantined or killed. They are also prone to the parasite *Gyrodactylus salaris*, which has meant that whole river systems in Norway have had to be poisoned with the insecticide rotenone[85,86] and restocked."

– Charles Clover[87]

"Increasingly, we will be faced with a choice: whether to keep the oceans for wild fish or farmed fish. Farming domesticated species in close proximity with wild fish will mean that domesticated fish always win. Nobody in the world of policy appears to be asking what is best for society, wild fish or farmed fish." – Charles Clover[88]

"Scottish Salmon and sea trout are under constant threat. We are here to protect them.

"The problems facing our migratory fish are real, present and increasing. Marine survival for salmon remains at historically low levels – now for

---

85 "In California in 1997, a lake that was a primary water source for 2,300 people was treated with rotenone in order to kill Northern Pike. The pike had been illegally introduced into the lake and were threatening to destroy prized salmon and trout fisheries. However the pesticide killed all the fish in the lake. The residents were forced to find an alternative water source, as the seven-mile lake was still contaminated six months later."
http://www.chm.bris.ac.uk/motm/rotenone/piscicide.html

86 Hulland, J. (2012). Rotenone to Eradicate Gyrodactylus salaris in Norway. The Fish Site. "Immediately after the treatment, the Vefsna will be entirely devoid of all life, both fish and invertebrate."
http://www.thefishsite.com/articles/1341/rotenone-to-eradicate-gyrodactylus-salaris-in-norway

87 Clover, C. (2006). The End of the Line: How Overfishing Is Changing the World and What We Eat. The New Press.

every 100 juvenile fish that go to sea, no more than five will return. It is vital that we do everything to ensure that the maximum number of wild smolts leave our rivers and reach the open ocean safely, and that as many returning adults as possible reach their natal rivers.

- Salmon abundance (adults returning to our coasts) is now less than 20% of that seen 50 years ago
- Fish farming is destroying west Highland and Hebridean wild salmon and sea trout stocks and iconic sea trout fisheries ..."

– Salmon & Trout Association[88]

RECOMMENDED

Readers are directed to the websites of the Salmon & Trout Association www.salmon-trout.org, in particular their Scottish site www.salmon-troutscotland.org and Stand Up For Wild Salmon www.standupforwildsalmon.org.

The Sea Louse

The most widely publicised and debated of all salmon farm problems is the sea louse,[89] partly because they cause so much harm to salmon in farms and in the wild, but also because control methods and residues cause plenty of public concern.[90]

> "There is overwhelming scientific evidence that salmon farms pose a threat to wild salmon and sea trout. Salmon are currently farmed in open-net cages, which mean that only the netting separates farmed fish from wild. This allows parasites, disease, waste products and pesticides to flow freely into the wild and impact wild fish. And many fish farms are located close to estuaries important for wild salmon and sea trout, making interaction between farmed and wild fish inevitable." – Salmon & Trout Association[91]

Sea lice are small aquatic crustaceans of which several species infest the Atlantic salmon, but one *Lepeophtheirus salmonis* is the most usual parasite of salmon farmed in Britain. They attach themselves to young fishes, feeding on their surface mucus, skin and blood creating often large open wounds. Sea lice hang onto salmon, nibbling chunks out of them. Thus sea lice prevent healthy development and a severe infestation may lead to death. A salmon can be horribly infested with these animals, but as few as three lice can be fatal to a small fish.[92] Survivors of a sea louse attack become sickly, deformed and unfit for sale.

> "Salmon farming industry figures reveal Scottish regions where sea-lice are out of control on fish-farms salmon & trout association (Scotland) demands answers of SSPO and Scottish government. In June 2013 over one third of salmon farms (47 farms) on the Scottish mainland and in the Hebrides were

88 http://www.salmon-troutscotland.org
89 http://www.thefishsite.com/diseaseinfo/13/amoebic-gill-disease-agd
90 http://www.standupforwildsalmon.org/Home
91 http://www.standupforwildsalmon.org/Problems.html
92 Morton, A. & Routledge, R. (2005). Mortality rates for Juvenile Pink Oncorhynchus gorbushca and Chum O. keta salmon infested with Sea Lice Lepeophtheirus salmonis in the Broughton Archipelago. Alaska Fishery Research Bulletin, 11(2): 146-152.

in areas where average sea-lice numbers exceeded the industry's own limit for sea lice. In each of the previous five months at least one quarter (35 farms) were in this category." – Salmon & Trout Association[93]

"Just what is the issue with sea lice? As they migrate to sea, juvenile wild salmon and sea trout enter bays and sea lochs containing salmon farms that produce an abundance of juvenile sea lice many orders of magnitude above natural background levels. Young fish are not equipped to cope with sea lice and numerous studies have shown that high lice burdens can prove fatal. A recent exhaustive study[94] concluded that lice were responsible for 'a 39 per cent loss in salmon abundance'." – Salmon & Trout Association (Scotland)[95]

"The parasitic crustaceans were probably acquired during early marine migration in areas that host large aquaculture populations of domesticated salmon, which elevate local abundances of ectoparasitic copepods – particularly *Lepeophtheirus salmonis* [sea lice]. These results provide experimental evidence from a large marine ecosystem that parasites can have large impacts on fish recruitment, fisheries and conservation."

– Krkošek *et al.*, 2012[96]

Life of Salmon, Wild and Captive

The British Isles are home to just one species of salmon – Atlantic Salmon *Salmo Salar* – of which there are both wild and captive populations. Wild salmon lay their eggs in freshwater rivers. Young fishes pass though juvenile stages known as fry, parr and smoult, the last having undergone an adaptation process that will enable them to live in salt water. At this stage they migrate down their river of birth to the sea and head north to rich feeding grounds in the North Atlantic Ocean. There, preying on smaller fishes such as capelin, young herring and sand eels, they grow rapidly during their first year away from home, to a weight of up to four kilograms.

During the next summer some of these regular-sized adult salmon may return to spawn while others choose to stay a further two or more years at sea. These are the salmon adults that, when they return, may become the grand specimens prized by anglers. Eventually all return to their birth river to mate and re-run the salmon life cycle.

That is all fine until a fish farm is anchored in the path of a wild salmon (or sea trout) migration route. Because a fish farmer wishes to place his cages in an environment ideal for the culture of salmon, more often than not he decides his farm should be where, not uncoincidentally, the wild salmon are. This creates a conflict of interests.

"A wealth of scientific evidence points to a clear link between salmon farms and adverse impacts on wild salmon and sea trout, both from the transfer of disease and parasites, especially sea lice, and the interbreeding of escaped farmed salmon with wild stocks, thus potentially endangering gene pools.

93 http://www.salmon-trout.org/news_item.asp?news_id=275
94 Krkošek et al., 2012.
95 http://www.salmon-troutscotland.org/fish_farming.asp
96 Krkošek, M., Revie, C.W., Gargan, P.G., Skilbrei, O.T., Finstad, B & Todd, C.D. (2013). Impact of parasites on salmon recruitment in the Northeast Atlantic Ocean. Proceedings of the Royal Society Biological Sciences, 280(1750): 20122359.

All initiatives over the last two decades to promote dialogue between wild fish interests and the fish farming industry have produced almost nothing of value to protect wild fish from farming impact. Consequently there has been a marked and disproportionate decline in rod catches in the west Highlands and Islands compared to the rest of Scotland." – Salmon & Trout Association (Scotland)[97]

We know well enough what happens when land based farmer plants a monoculture crop or keeps large numbers of stock all together. Pests and diseases can have a high old time in and on the greatest gift of all time: perfect conditions for setting up home, all the food they can eat and, because they are all gathered together in huge numbers of the same species, the ideal conditions for reproduction.

So it is for farmed fishes, as the salmon farmer knows only too well. They soon pick up ghastly parasites and horrible diseases which multiply joyfully among the crowded salmon, their abundant home, food source and repro-dome, passing from fish to fish with the greatest of ease until all are infested or infected. He can't sell fish that has been nibbled till deformed by horrible parasitic creatures or are weakened and emaciated by sickness. His only recourse is to apply pesticides and medicines with all the additional problems they bring of cost, contamination and residues.

Not everyone agrees that trouble on the fish farm lead to trouble in the wild. Some will deny it, while others, sidestepping any evidence, assert that the matter is an even-handed controversy. Certainly, the wild fishes and natural plankton were the original sources of pests and diseases that found their way to the farmed fishes, but the fish farm crams thousand of their host together, enabling them to run riot. Wild salmon passing close to the cages full of infected salmon, or farmed salmon escaping and joining the wild ones, means that parasites and diseases are exchanged and the wild salmon stocks suffer so badly that eventually entire populations may be exterminated.

Aquaculturalists seem to have greatest difficulty conceding the fact that wild salmon stocks are dwindling or that that is because of their fish farms' presence in wild waters. Remember this from Chapter 1?

Tom Heap: "Scott, are lice from your farms killing wild salmon?"

Scott Landsburgh: "No. I wouldn't say so. I mean, there's a lot of discussion about it but ... um ... there's no empirical evidence that suggests that that's the case." – *Countryfile*[98]

From that you would think there's nothing to argue about (and they would rather we didn't). The Scottish Salmon Producers' Organisation (SSPO) is confident that the sea louse problem does not start with the fish farms, but that's the opposite of what scientific research has concluded from the empirical evidence that the Landsburgh claimed does not exist. Salmon producers skirt around the reality of the situation with fancy publicity:

"We have worked closely with many river owners to enhance the Wild Salmon stocks in local rivers. By providing a year round supply of

97 http://www.salmon-troutscotland.org/fish_farming.asp
98 BBC1, 1 December 2013.

> consistent quality Scottish Salmon, we are reducing the demand for the scarce Wild Salmon where stocks are depleting."
>
> – Wester Ross Fisheries Ltd.[99]

How very generous they are, seemingly. Apparently the fish farmers are caringly mitigating for wild salmon populations depleted by their own activities (though they don't quite put it that way). Some companies demonstrate a slightly more realistic outlook.

> "Sea lice management is important from both a welfare and cost perspective and to ensure that sea lice on farms do not have a negative impact on wild salmonid stocks and other wild species." – Marine Harvest[100]

Ah, so Marine Harvest acknowledge that there is at least the possibility of "...a negative impact on wild salmonid stocks."

Let's see what Scott Landsburgh's 'non-existent' empirical evidence really says about sea lice, fish farms and wild salmon.

> "A 10-week study in the Broughton Archipelago found sea lice were 8.8 times more abundant on wild fish near farms holding adult salmon and 5.0 times more abundant on wild fish near farms holding smolts than in areas distant from salmon farms. Sea lice abundance was near zero in all areas without salmon farms. The evidence from this control–impact study points to a relationship between salmon farms and sea lice on adjacent, wild, juvenile salmon." – Morton *et al.*, 2004[101]

> "Marine salmon farming has been correlated with parasitic sea lice infestations and concurrent declines of wild salmonids." – Krkošek, Lewis & Volpe, 2005[102]

> "We show that recurrent louse infestations of wild juvenile pink salmon (*Oncorhynchus gorbuscha*), all associated with salmon farms, have depressed wild pink salmon populations and placed them on a trajectory toward rapid local extinction." – Krkošek *et al.*, 2007[103]

> "Wild salmon stocks in Canadian coastal waters are being severely affected by parasites from fish farms. So intense are these infestations that some populations of salmon are at risk of extinction." – Andrew A. Rosenberg, 2008[104]

---

99 http://www.wrs.co.uk/environment [Do not confuse with Wester Ross Fisheries Trust, advocates for wild fishes.]

100 Marine Harvest Annual Report, 2013. Leading the Blue Revolution. http://hugin.info/209/R/1781099/609198.pdf

101 Morton, A., Routledge, R., Peet, C. & Ladwig, A. (2004). Sea lice (Lepeophtheirus salmonis) infection rates on juvenile pink (Oncorhynchus gorbuscha) and chum (Oncorhynchus keta) salmon in the nearshore marine environment of British Columbia, Canada. Canadian Journal of Fisheries and Aquatic Sciences, 61: 147–157.

102 Krkošek, Lewis, M.A. and Volpe, J.P. (2005). Transmission dynamics of parasitic sea lice from farm to wild salmon. Proceedings of the Royal Society Biological Sciences, 272(1564): 689–696.

103 Krkošek, M., Ford, S.J., Morton, A., Lele, S., Myers, R.A. & Lewis, M.A. (2007). Declining Wild Salmon Populations in Relation to Parasites from Farm Salmon. Science, 318(5857): 1772-1775.

104 Rosenberg, A.A. (2008). The price of lice. Nature, 451: 23–24

> "Fishes farmed in sea pens may become infested by parasites from wild fishes and in turn become point sources for parasites. Sea lice are the most significant parasitic pathogen in salmon farming in Europe and the Americas, are estimated to cost the world industry €300 million a year and may also be pathogenic to wild fishes under natural conditions." – Mark J. Costello, 2009[105]

> "The parasitic crustaceans were probably acquired during early marine migration in areas that host large aquaculture populations of domesticated salmon ..." – Krkošek *et al.*, 2012[106]

Here we have just six out of a wealth of peer-refereed papers published in top scientific journals (including the prestigious *Proceedings of the Royal Society, Science* and *Nature*), which should provide sufficient empirical evidence to counter any denials by the SSPO and cunningly worded fish farm publicity that seems to say a lot whilst either meaning something quite different, or very little.

The south Skye lochs used to contain small fish farms, closed some years ago because (allegedly – some deny this) they became overrun by sea lice (below). They have been free of farmed salmon, sea lice

Unforeseen Ecological Consequences

We often discover (though more often, in our ignorance, we don't even notice) consequences of our rash activities we have failed to predict. Nature is not a simplistic assortment of individuals or species but a mind-bogglingly complicated network of interacting organisms all working together in various forms of symbiosis.[107] Crashing populations of wild salmon and trout are devastating for an apparently completely unrelated species, the freshwater pearl mussel ***Margaritifera margaritifera***.

The minute larvae (glochidia) of this extraordinary animal must attach themselves to the gills of juvenile salmonid fishes during the early part of their life cycle and be transported to suitable places for them to complete their up to 130-years. No salmonids = no mussels.

Mussel populations have been devastated by collecting – these days it's poaching – and pollution, and there are very few places where they now live. The authorities are cautious not to implicate salmon farming in the decline of the freshwater pearl mussel, but, for instance, JNCC lists pearl-fishing, pollution, acidification, organic enrichment, siltation, river engineering, and *declining salmonid stocks* as causes.[108] Concentrating on illegal pearl fishing, SNH has yet to acknowledge this obvious cause of near

---

105 Costello, M.J. (2009). How sea lice from salmon farms may cause wild salmonid declines in Europe and North America and be a threat to fishes elsewhere. Proceedings of the Royal Society Biological Sciences, 276(1672): 3385-3394.

106 Krkošek, M., Revie, C.W., Gargan, P.G., Skilbrei, O.T., Finstad, B & Todd, C.D. (2013). Impact of parasites on salmon recruitment in the Northeast Atlantic Ocean. Proceedings of the Royal Society Biological Sciences, 280(1750): 20122359.

107 Defined at the beginning of Chapter 1.

108 http://jncc.defra.gov.uk/protectedsites/sacselection/species.asp?FeatureIntCode=s1029

extinction of the mussels.[109] Obvious? We know, from plentiful peer reviewed research, that a proven major cause of decline in wild salmonid stocks is the presence of salmon farms situated in the path of migrating salmon and their generous donation of sea lice. We also know that 2 + 2 = 4. Catch up SNH!

Amoebic gill disease

Another major source of consternation on Scottish fish farms is the potentially fatal amoebic gill disease (AMG)[110] which, once it gets a hold, can spread rapidly through entire farms causing massive losses. AMG has only recently found its way to Scotland, having first been a big problem in Tasmania where it has been known to cost aquaculture up to A$230M (£126M) annually.

> "GRIEG Seafood, one of Scotland's big five salmon farmers, has lost one-third of its latest harvest to amoebic gill disease, the ailment that is set to cost the industry more than £30 million in lost revenue." – Steven Vass[111]

Therapeutants: Pesticides & 'Medicines'

As in agriculture, when monocultures foster the proliferation of pests and diseases, humans attempt the counter attack, which traditionally is chemical. Each problem has its individual solution and since sea lice infestation was the earliest to trouble Scottish aquaculture, the remedy has enjoyed an interesting evolution. There is no need to go into detail here because an excellent history of sea louse treatment is provided by Wikipedia[112] (*Drugs and vaccines*).

It used to be common practice to dunk infested fishes in a vast bath of pesticide. This is still carried out when infestations get out of hand, but the modern way is to administer a drug in feed pellets. This of course – we have learnt this lesson, haven't we? – is precisely the way that we caused the emergence of multiple resistance farmyard disease bacteria, by subjecting them to a selection pressure that obliged them to evolve rapidly. But there you are: that's the way they choose to do it, partly because an infestation of sea lice can be an intractable predicament with no total cure (in net-cage aquaculture as currently conducted) leading to a loss of product up with which the industry cannot put.

Organophosphates,[113] notably Dichlorvos, are thankfully no longer widely used. However, the water-soluble Azamethiphos (Salmosan®) is said to be broken down rapidly in the environment, so I suppose that's OK(?)

---

109 http://www.snh.gov.uk/about-scotlands-nature/species/invertebrates/freshwater-invertebrates/freshwater-pearl-mussel/
110 http://www.thefishsite.com/diseaseinfo/13/amoebic-gill-disease-agd
111 Gill disease to cost salmon farmers £30m. The Herald, 19 January 2013.
http://www.heraldscotland.com/business/markets-economy/gill-disease-to-cost-salmon-farmers-30m.19956340
112 http://en.wikipedia.org/wiki/Sea_louse#Drugs_and_vaccines
113 Remember the plight of farmers who used OP sheep dip?

The Pyrethroid Cypermethrin has fallen out of favour, though its 'safer' cousin Deltamethrin (Alphamax® – not to be confused with the synonymous male hormone supplement or erotic PVC figurines!) is still used and said by some companies to be 'safe'.

However, the drug of choice has for some time been one or other of a group known as the Avermectins. Some years ago, Ivermectin – which is used elsewhere for worming cattle – was used on salmon, but this neurotoxin proved not entirely satisfactory (it has a tendency to kill fishes). The alternative Emamectin Benzoate was tried, found to be less piscitoxic and is now used as a constituent of fish feed widely under the trade mark SLICE®. The drug passes from gut to tissues where it is absorbed by feeding sea lice.

SLICE® has its disadvantages. SLICE® leaves the system in excess feed and faeces where, we are told by SEPA,[114] "... most releases will end up in sediments or particulate material. It is usually dispersed fairly efficiently, but is otherwise not particularly mobile." I think SEPA's second sentence means that, after it leaves a salmon in its faeces, SLICE® stays on the seabed (in the yukky gunge that builds up there), though some of it might wash away to become somebody else's problem (see Scottish Government quotations below).

SLICE® can also leave the system in fish tissue, which is, as it happens, off to market to be eaten by humans.[115] SEPA is particularly non-committal on this.

So SLICE® accumulates in sediments beneath and adjacent to fish cages, potentially affecting wild crustaceans and it is toxic to fish, birds, mammals and marine invertebrates. Otherwise SLICE® is just fine, so don't worry, the government has it all in hand.

> "There is very little information available on the environmental fate and ecological effects of emamectin benzoate in the marine environment.
>
> "The organisms most likely to be affected by emamectin benzoate are those closely associated with the sediment as emamectin has low water solubility and a high potential to be adsorbed and bound to suspended particulate material. Much of the emamectin reaching the sediments will be associated with particulate material in the form of fish faeces and uneaten fish food. Emamectin remains in the sediments for a considerable period of time having a half life (i.e. the time taken for the concentration to diminish by 50%) of around 175 days.
>
> "The environmental risk of emamectin benzoate to the marine environment is considered to be low to moderate. However, there is relatively little information available on the toxicity of this chemical to marine benthic invertebrates in particular, and little is known about the potential long-term impacts of this chemical on the marine environment." – The Scottish Government[116]

---

114 http://apps.sepa.org.uk/spripa/Pages/SubstanceInformation.aspx?pid=171
115 See Final SLICE® Thoughts below ("The U.S. Food and Drug Administration ... etc.").
116 Effects of Discharges of Medicines and Chemicals from Aquaculture – sea lice medicines http://www.scotland.gov.uk/Publications/2002/08/15170/9409

It comes as no surprise when we hear ecologists' concerns that SLICE® could have devastating (fatal) effects on marine crustaceans other than lice, for instance crabs, lobsters, prawns and others. If you read the label on Syngenta's Proclaim® insecticide – which contains 5% Emamectin Benzoate[117] – you are left in no doubt of its toxicity, which might well affect marine crustaceans if it came into contact with them, for instance on or in the sea bed beneath a fish farm:

> "ENVIRONMENTAL HAZARDS This pesticide is toxic to fish, birds, mammals, and aquatic invertebrates. Drift and runoff may be hazardous to aquatic organisms in neighboring areas. Do not apply directly to water, to areas where surface water is present or to intertidal areas below the mean high water mark." – Proclaim® Insecticide product label.

When it comes to advantages, SLICE® certainly kills sea lice, but it does so incompletely and quite often sea lice infestations still get out of hand in spite of measures to overcome them.

> "Yet again, salmon farming industry figures reveal that sea lice numbers are out of control in parts of the west coast and western isles. The Salmon & Trout Association (Scotland) calls on Ministers to show leadership with decisive action in Wester Ross where lice numbers have been consistently over thresholds for a full year. The latest aggregated sea lice data, published by the Scottish Salmon Producers Organisation (SSPO), shows that in the fourth quarter of 2013 sea lice numbers on farmed salmon were massively out of control in a number of areas." – Salmon & Trout Association[118]

SLICE® – Points to Ponder

- When you next walk through a cow field, observe the condition of the pancakes at your feet. If 'healthy' they will be riddled with the burrows of coprophagous[119] beetles and fly larvae and perhaps topped by a mushroom or two belonging to a coprophilous fungus that are all feeding voraciously on this nutritious dung. Good cow pats like this soon disintegrate and disappear after a couple of weeks.
- However, you sometimes come across a field full of cow pats with a hard or leathery crust, no sign of burrowing dung-eating creatures and often with a cap of mosses and other plants growing on them. Cow pats like this might have been there for a year or more, because they have not undergone decomposition. No self respecting arthropod will eat them (or dies if it tries) because the cows that deposited them had been dosed with another Avermectin, this time Ivermectin, which is fed to cattle to reduce infestations of gut parasites. It persists in cow pats, preventing insects in particular from going to work on them by killing them. Remember the half life of Emamectin Benzoate – 175 days? No wonder.

---

117 Fish farm SLICE® is applied as Emamectin Benzoate 0.2% (a reduction that does not change its chemical properties).

118 http://www.salmon-troutscotland.org/news_item.asp?news_id=297

119 Coprophagous: dung-eating; Coprophilous: dung-liking.

- The U.S. Food and Drug Administration has listed Emamectin benzoate as an Unapproved Drug that should not be used on fish destined for consumption in the U.S.A. What about us then?

Biological Control

Some salmon farm companies acknowledge that sea lice are not under control by chemical means and that biological control, if effective, might be better for PR anyway, after many years of criticism over the control methods they have employed so far. Some companies have included 'cleaner fish' in their anti sea lice programmes, adding wrasse species and, recently, lumpsuckers to salmon cages where, it is said, they peck the lice off their victims or food.

Wester Ross Fisheries Ltd. obtain their wrasse in large numbers from the wild[120]. When a production cycle has been completed and the salmon harvested, the wrasse are all killed. Then a new batch of wild wrasse has to be collected and their fate is also to be killed at the end of a cycle. Any biologist will find the flaw in this methodology quite obvious!

However, the Machrihanish Environmental Research Laboratory (MERL)[121] in Argyll, Scotland is working hard at breeding wrasse specifically for the aquaculture industry.[122] Whether or not cleaner fish will take the place of toxic chemical remedies has yet to become clear. It is not easy to find your way through the hype of a method that has been proclaimed for at least ten years or so. If it's the cleaner fish method works, why do new fish farm proposals[123] include SLICE® and not wrasse? All credit to Marine Harvest who are seriously trying it out and collaborating with MERL on the research.

120 Personal communication, Ullapool, 16 January 2014.
121 http://www.fishresearch.co.uk/facilities/merl
122 http://www.fishresearch.co.uk/news/73_wrasse_a_green_alternative_for_sea_lice_removal
123 e.g. Hjaltland Seafood's planning application 14/01467/FUL.
http://wam.highland.gov.uk/wam/applicationDetails.do?activeTab=documents&keyVal=N3VEIBIH09K00

Chapter 6
MARINE POLLUTION

ECHOES OF BLACKADDER II

(*see Preface opener*)

A FICTITIOUS INTERVIEW with a made-up spokesperson representing the nonexistent Association of Scottish Salmon Farmers (ASSF).

Interviewer: But what happens to the fish feed your salmon eat? What happens to the faeces?

Emma McTynn (ASSF): Um, well, what we are talking about in aquacultural effluent treatment terms is the latest in sustainable, government approved net-cage/open-water interface multiple orifices combined with a sustainable, self-regulating autoflush distribution and disposal system.

Interviewer: You mean your salmon crap in the loch?

Emma McTynn: No. The ... the ... er ... the public don't really understand the complexities of sustainable aquaculture. All of our sustainable operations are SEPA-approved.

Interviewer: Your salmon *do* crap in the loch, don't they?

Emma McTynn: Well, kind of, a bit, but not very much, and it's all washed away, sustainably, out to sea.

Interviewer (*to camera*): Their salmon crap in the loch.

Emma McTynn: There's no empirical evidence that suggests any harm to the environment. We are a 'Best Practice' industry. All of our operations are sustainable. We've won awards, you know.

Interviewer (*to camera*): For filling the loch with crap? Thank you, Ms McTynn.

Emma McTynn: ... and anyway, all of our operations are SEPA-approved ... sustainable ... and ... er ... gulp ... only doing my job. Our industry *creates* jobs, you know, and we've given away lots of money to the *community*, to fund a youth club and ... and ... and ...

– Biographical Note –

When not representing the ASSF, Emma helps out on her brother Ivor's dairy farm and plays in a traditional dance band The Ceilidhsides with Della Methrin, Sally 'Sal' Mosan and Richard Lorvoss.

Emma recently got engaged to fish farm manager Max, who she lovingly describes as "a proper alpha male".

(KEY at end of chapter)

> "You show me pollution and I will show you people who are not paying their own way, people who are stealing from the public, people who are getting the public to pay their costs of production. All environmental pollution is a subsidy." – Robert F. Kennedy Jr.

> "They claimed that the environmental standards were absurdly strict and were costing the regions jobs and hurting the economy (the polluters' favorite mantra)." – Donald Prothero[124]

Last Ordures Please!

For me, marine pollution is the most persuasive argument against net-cage salmon farming (as currently conducted). Please note that I have been, and will continue to be, specific about the aquaculture method under discussion using the carefully constructed description: *net-cage salmon farming as currently conducted* (see Chapter 3).

I wouldn't write what follows if I didn't think what I have to say is more-or-less correct, but I don't claim to absolutely right on every point, firstly because I'm a scientist and scientists' conclusions are always provisional and subject to revision if/when new evidence arrives; and second, because I'm relatively new to fish-farm discussion and am still learning about the subject and its pros and cons. My position on any controversial subject is like that of John Maynard Keynes when he (is reported to have) said:

> "When my information changes, I alter my conclusions. What do you do, sir?"
>
> – John Maynard Keynes[125]

So if anyone can persuade me that any of what follows is untrue or inaccurate, then I will alter my conclusions. I've done that before – painful as it was, but getting less so the more often I do it – and I can and will change my mind again, when (but only when) new facts or updated information make a change of mind the honest recourse.

Objectors to what I say should note that since my conclusions are based on the best evidence available, *alternative evidence* must be provided before I will consider changing those conclusions. I will refuse to adjust my conclusions if presented only with dogmatic assertions, illogical contentions or out-and-out lies, the improper sort of 'evidence' sometimes irrationally blurted out by zealous proponents of salmon farming (... as currently conducted in Scotland).

I can't be more reasonable than that.

NETS full of HOLES are the problem and POLLUTION is the foundation of my criticisms of net-cage salmon farming (as currently conducted). I maintain that fish farm pollution can be eliminated at a stroke using non-net, solid walled containers, though not without considerable expenditure on the part of the aquaculture industry. So what? For the sake of our already beleaguered marine environment, the industry –

124 Prothero, Donald R. (2013). Reality Check: How Science Deniers Threaten Our Future. Indiana University Press.
125 His reply to a criticism during the Great Depression of having changed his position on monetary policy.

proclaimed by Scottish Sea Farms Ltd to be *The Heart of the Community* – should be overjoyed to bear that cost. I will keep saying it:

Who should be paying to farm salmon safely?

1. The aquaculture industry that makes huge profits and holds massive financial resources?[126]
2. Their customers who want to eat their fish?
3. The tax-paying public (subsidy)?
4. Nature, obliged to endure the pollution load?[127]

Enlightenment Moment It was only relatively recently – after climbing the steep learning curve from knowledge-zero and thinking long and hard about fish farming – that it dawned on me that farmed salmon are kept in nets and that netting consists almost entirely of ...

HOLES

All of a sudden it became obvious to me that nets are just holes tied together with string and that it was important to keep this always in mind when considering and discussing net-cage fish farming. It is *the* fundamental flaw in the method.

Every earthworm knows about this and so should we:

- **Holes** are perforations, cavities, voids, fissures, passages, vents, lacunae, clefts, chinks and apertures through which stuff, including worms, may freely pass.
- **Holes** do not obstruct, block, hinder, occlude, plug, check, choke, stop, thwart or impede the passage of stuff (including worms, of course), notably if the stuff under consideration is smaller than the holes, or dissolved or suspended in water.
- Because of the holes of which they entirely consist (apart from the string that ties the holes together), nets let stuff pass through and they let stuff escape that perhaps ought to be kept in.
- The main component of Scottish salmon farms – as currently constructed – is ten or twelve nets full of fishes.
- Therefore ... *readers are encouraged to reach their own conclusions.*

Fish excrement

A major outrage the fish farmers keep quiet about, the authorities tend to underplay and of which most of the public are blissfully unaware is the tonnes and tonnes and tonnes of fish FAECES dumped at sea through the HOLES in the fish farm nets. I don't know precisely how many tonnes, but I daresay it could be calculated. Even a

126 e.g. Marine Harvest: Revenue £1.53 billion; Total Assets £2.16 billion; Total Equity £1.03 billion. Marine Harvest, Annual Report, 2010.

127 Thanks to Roger Cottis for originally formulating this mantra.

rough idea of how many tonnes would be a very large amount of ordure and, since it all goes straight into the sea, also a very large amount of pollution.

That's right: as already discussed in Chapter 1, Scottish fish farms quietly dispose of *all* of their waste in the sea. I can't think of any other industry or community service that is allowed to do such a thing – can you?

Organic waste may sometimes be inadvertently let loose in the natural environment, sometimes with the most unexpected consequences. Here is a startling example that we should take as a warning.

A Cautionary Tale

Recent research[128] has detected a chain of apparently unconnected events that link sugar cane farming in Queensland, Australia to appalling coral kills on the Great Barrier Reef. Cause and effect combine make a bizarre story.

- Queensland farmers, as is conventional, applied fertiliser to their sugar cane crops.
- Rain and river floods washed a proportion of that fertiliser off the land into streams and rivers that empty into the Coral Sea.
- Microscopic marine plants (the phytoplankton) thrived on elevated nutrients inadvertently provided by sugar cane farmers ...
- ... leading to a population explosion in the marine phytoplankton ('algal bloom').
- The larvae of the Crown-of-Thorns starfish feed on the phytoplankton, which became more plentiful and, therefore, better fed than usual, the baby starfish enjoyed a greatly enhanced survival rate ...
- ... which caused a population explosion among Crown-of-Thorns adults.
- Crown-of-Thorns starfish adults feed on coral polyps ...
- ... so the corals got grazed to death ...

... all because of organic excess unintentionally finding its way from far inland into the sea. Population explosions of Crown-of-Thorns starfish *Acanthaster planci* since the mid 1980s have been estimated to account for 42 per cent of coral damage on the Great Barrier Reef. This is a complicated example of catastrophic environmental nutrient overload, known as *eutrophication* (explained below).

We must wonder what will the consequences be of siting fish farms along the entire coast of west Scotland and allowing them to dispose of all their organic waste in the sea, untreated? Admittedly an individual fish farm doesn't occupy a lot of space compared with the area of sea – particularly evident if you use Google Earth to view fish-farms in their geographical context – but even so, what is the fate of the nutrient rich effluent that constantly oozes out of ten to twelve net-cages, and what must be the ecological consequences?

Apparently SEPA knows and is confident that no harm will ensue, because it gives out licenses to aquaculture companies on the understanding that they aren't going to pollute Scotland's sea lochs. They run computer models to prove the environmental

128 Fabricius, K. E., Okaji, K. & De'ath, G. (2010). Coral Reefs. Three lines of evidence to link outbreaks of the crown-of-thorns seastar Acanthaster planci to the release of larval food limitation. 29(3), 593-605.

safety of net-cage salmon farming, so surely it must be OK? I contend that SEPA's limits are too generous; too optimistic that fish farm effluent will cause no lasting or significant harm.

Let me put it this way: With reference to my biological experience and common sense, *I have yet to be convinced* that the limits SEPA set on net-cage salmon farm effluent are realistic. Why not contain all that muck in the first place, rather than letting it loose in Scottish sea lochs where it is unlikely to be beneficial, and more than likely, detrimental? Why wait until, as has already happened on the Great Barrier Reef, immeasurable irreparable damage has been done?

➔ If salmon farming is to have a truly sustainable future, salmon should be contained and their excrement controlled. This can be done and would be done if the authorities were to instruct the aquaculture industry to comply with new environmentally considerate standards. Then fish farmers could justifiably advertise that they belong to a 'Best Practice' industry (currently it is no more than a shallow PR boast). 🡐

Having watched it happen, I have first-hand experience of what nutrient enriched sea water can do to sensitive marine life. When I worked at the Department of Biology, University of York we maintained some sea-water tanks in the laboratories for undergraduate teaching. From time to time some of the tanks would be stocked with all manner of sea creatures, a biodiversity collection sent down from Scotland (Millport), while others contained large numbers of common crabs, mussels or sea anemones for students' research projects.

It was my job to drive a Land Rover stacked with large plastic bottles to the coast every couple of months to collect sea water with which to clean out and top up the system. A few scary winter visits, when I could tell my life was in danger from capricious waves, I decided to go somewhere safer than Scarborough sea front. Robin Hood's Bay was chosen. When I poured the new water into the lab tanks the sea anemones in particular showed their great distaste by retracting and never waving their tentacles again. It seemed that the water I had collected was contaminated, which nobody expected of RHB. After some inquiry, it turned out that a pig farm inland was leaking slurry into a stream that emptied into the bay and that made our captive anemones terminally unhappy. You will be pleased to know that we worked out how to obtain cleaner water that was acceptable to lab anemones, though never so clear and sweet as West Highland sea loch water (away from fish farms).

Experience also informs me that, on land at least, probably elsewhere, most plants and most plant communities exist on very low concentrations of nutrients (actually often very low). In natural communities, such as woodland, plant roots are not the main organs of nutrient uptake. Fungi do the hard work of obtaining nutrients for plants (phosphorus in particular, since it is almost immobile in soil and roots can't reach it unaided), handing them over to their 'hosts' via combined exchange organs in roots. This alliance is called mycorrhiza (Greek: fungus-root), an example of symbiosis, in which two or more organisms work intimately together to the benefit of one, both or all of them. Symbioses of this sort are of particular benefit to the multi-species communities of which they part. Woodland is founded on and driven by mycorrhiza, many plants and many fungi working together in a sort of living mosaic that benefits all.

When fertiliser is added to mycorrhizal communities the symbiosis breaks down. Plants and fungi that have specific relationships lose touch with one another and many disappear from the community. Those that are less reliant on mycorrhiza then thrive, so a simplified community forms that consists of non-mycorrhizal plants, low-dependency mycorrhizal plants and low specificity 'weed' fungi. The ecosystem has become biologically impoverished and you can probably imagine that, thanks to human depredations, such ecosystems are widespread.

Even though scientists have shown how symbiotic relationships work, in isolation and in ecological communities, they are not well understood by scientists themselves, though their importance has been stated frequently. Such ideas have yet to find their way into the public consciousness, and until they do ignorant humans will continue cause untold harm to nature. Processes such as symbiosis are vitally important, but that about which people know nothing gets overlooked.

"We see only what we have names for." – Garrett Hardin[129]

We see biodiversity and ecosystem declines clearly enough on land, but they are less easy to observe at sea. We have all experienced murky seas that help us appreciate the crystal clear (did I hear someone say 'pristine'?) waters of the western Highlands. Similar consequences are likely under water if low nutrient high biodiversity marine ecosystems become similarly overloaded with nutrients. It seems very likely that fish farm effluent will eventually have – is already having? – a noticeable detrimental effect on clean sea lochs. It's called pollution, a word we should not stint from using when we talk about salmon farming (as currently conducted using net-cages that allow all effluent to pass through the holes in them into the sea).

I think we could now usefully re-read a passage quoted in the Preface.

> "This year [2000], salmon farms will produce 7,500 tons of nitrogen, equivalent to the annual sewage from 3.2 million people, and 1,240 tons of phosphorus, comparable to sewage from 9.4 million people. The ecological result is effectively greater than the sewage produced by Scotland's 5.1 million humans." – Dr Malcolm MacGarvin[130]

Such statistics soon become out-of-date. Because more and more fish farms are being installed, they are unlikely to become less alarming! Since 2000, Salmon farms have increased in number, size and productivity, and in 2012 the Scottish Government published its ambition to double national salmon output by 2020. It does not look good for the Scottish marine environment and here is why:

Pollution – Eutrophication

Environmental nutrient enrichment is known as eutrophication, from the Greek for overfed ('good-feeding' – imagine an overweight person). Nutrients are plentiful to excessive: overloaded. Thus, a nutrient overloaded ecosystem might be described as

129 Hardin, G. (1999). *The Ostrich Factor: Our Population Myopia*. Oxford University Press.
130 Quoted by *Telegraph* columnist Charles Clover, author of book and film concerned about overfishing *The End of the Line*. http://www.telegraph.co.uk/news/uknews/1355936/Pollution-from-fish-farms-as-bad-as-sewage.html

eutrophic. In such circumstances some species flourish whilst others decline and disappear due to, among other factors, competition, and the ecosystem becomes simplified, more uniform and less diverse than formerly. Though well fed, a eutrophic ecosystem is considered ecologically impoverished due to its reduced biodiversity.

At the opposite end of the food availability continuum is oligotrophic ('few-feeding' – imagine a skinny, underfed person). Nutrients are limited and hard to obtain unless specialised ecological services are available, such as are provided on land by mycorrhiza. Despite being poorly provided with nutrients, biodiversity is usually high in oligotrophic ecosystems.

We can all agree that an oligotrophic Highland lochan with white water lilies, bogbean, water lobelia, quill- and bladderworts, with newts, whirligig beetles and dragonflies is preferable by far to a noisome eutrophic pond full of blanket weed. Add fertiliser run-off or fish farm waste to the former and you'll turn it into the latter.

In between oligotrophic and eutrophic is mesotrophic ('middle-feeding' – body form just right). Nutrient supply adequate, but not overloading.

Oligotrophic and mesotrophic are natural states for natural ecosystems in which biodiversity is often high to very high. Even rain forest, with its high biodiversity and productivity, functions on little in the way of nutrients and a lot by way of biological interaction. The eutrophic condition occurs only when an otherwise healthy ecosystem gets loaded with nutrient enrichment substances, such as fertiliser run-off or sewage. If an ecosystem gets deluged with high-organic effluent or similar some (usually a few) species thrive and multiply, often out competing sensitive or less adaptable members of the community which becomes simplified and bloated. Familiar examples of such occurrences would be blanket weed in ponds and rivers and, of course, toxic algal blooms. We all – including owners of garden fish ponds, swimmers who encounter a 'red tide' and divers who prefer their coral reefs alive – usually agree:

oligotrophic good – mesotrophic OK – eutrophic bad

You should by now understand why net-cage fish farming might be harming marine ecosystems, by cumulative organic pollution (and that is not all – read on). Eutrophic waters are visually indistinguishable from clean oligotrophic waters, until the development of a bloom that makes the water murky or otherwise obviously contaminated. Dissolved enrichment is in itself generally imperceptible, made visible by its consequences. I expect that the sugar cane eutrophication that encouraged the Great Barrier Reef phytoplankton to proliferate was not visible until other changes, higher up the chain of consequence were spotted, such as a plague of starfish or dead corals.

Therefore, it would seem to be sensible not to release fish farm effluent into the sea and to devise methods for containing it. This has been done and is being done around the world, and should be applied to Scottish salmon farms forthwith (see Chapter 8).

Pollution – Sedimentation

Sediments cloud the water, settle and smother living creatures. Wildlife stifled by sediments dies and ecosystems become simplified – biodiversity reduced. Fish faeces become sedimentary fragments of all sizes and they settle to the sea bed. Mobile animals might be able leave the area when fragments of muck persistently land on them while sedentary animals and plants must stay put, choke and die.

Certain specialist organisms thrive in the sludge that builds up under a fish farm. Small worms of the genus *Capitella* that love to feed on detritus can become amazingly numerous, wiggling as only worms can in a dense, stinking mat of the filamentous bacterium *Beggiatoa*, that also thrives in such conditions. *Beggiatoa* is an anaerobic organism that loves to live where oxygen is in such short supply that most life forms would suffocate (as they do). It gets its energy by reducing sulphur, so the mat evolves hydrogen sulphide, which as you know smells of rotten eggs and is poisonous. As you can imagine, the sea bed beneath a fish farm, where a lot of the fish faeces settles, is a hostile environment for most sea life.

We ordinary folk don't visit such places a great deal, but numerous divers and remote camera operators have taken a look on our behalf. Their descriptions and pictures of the sea bed, not only directly beneath but outwards to quite a distance away, belie the muttered protestations of the fish farmers that their installations are clean. This is a subject about which they say very little and change the subject when others raise it for discussion, because there is nothing they can do about it as long as they keep their salmon in open-weave cages; and they don't want to have to be told they must change their methodologies because it would inconvenience them a great deal.

My heart bleeds for them.

Pollution – Excess Fish Feed

The aquaculture industry is doing a reasonable job of cutting down on what used to be a major organic pollutant, excess fish feed. In the past, it used to be shovelled in at the top of the cages to drift slowly down the water column. If it was not eaten *en route* by a salmon, it fell out of the bottom of the cage to pile up among the fallen faeces on the sea bed. This was wasteful and costing the industry money, so they had every good reason to pull their socks up and they did. Now, fewer pellets fall out of the cages because inputs are managed and outputs monitored. A large container barge is anchored adjacent to the cages, linked to each by a plastic pipe through which feed pellets are fed. Cameras under the cages watch for a 'rain' of pellets so that inputs may be limited when necessary. They tell us it works, and of course, because such systems save money, I expect we can believe them.

Does feed input-output monitoring provide the solution to the pollution problem? I think not. Some pellets evade monitoring and still reach the sea bed, but more importantly, a lot of the feed that enters the cages at the top leaves through the holes in the nets as fish poo, all of which – as we have seen – is dumped in the sea. The pollution problem will persist as long as the salmon are kept in nets containers full of holes.

Pollution – Pesticides, 'Drugs' & 'Medicines'

The fate of Emamectin Benzoate in SLICE® has already been discussed (Chapter 5). Other sea louse control pesticides, mostly no longer in use (we hope), might also emerge from the system in fish faeces and fish meat. We must also consider their derivatives, breakdown products the structure and toxicities of which will be enormously variable. Some will be safe and others hazardous.

Some drugs will pass through the fish unutilised and unchanged by digestive processes, while others will already have begun to decompose to simplified chemical subunits. Do we know which and how much? The curious reader may investigate.

Amoebic Gill Disease is generally treated in a bath of dilute hydrogen peroxide (H_2O_2) which is used at low concentrations and is rapidly denatured to water when disposed of. Not too worrying. No, it's SLICE® residues that concern us most in Scottish waters, so let's hope that SLICE® is as 'safe' as we are assured it is, or that its presence in the under-cage bacterial mat is not cumulative or harmful, and that if any comes out of fish farms in fish flesh, that it is, as we are assured by the Powers That Be, completely harmless when devoured by people.

I remain very uneasy.

Beneath & Beyond – the Fish Farm Footprint

With all that stuff dropping through the holes in the net you would expect some to hit the sea bed. What really happens? Organic waste, in vast quantities, piles up under a fish farm where some sort of decomposition process occurs. To begin with that is an aerobic process, with an array of bacteria and invertebrate animals beavering away, eating the muck and turning into something more-or-less pleasant and some of it washes away – out of mind.

As the muck pile deepens, changes happen, mainly the elimination of oxygen from the decomposition cycle. The system becomes anoxic and the few creatures that can continue decomposing are anaerobic – mostly the dense bacterial *Beggiatoa* mat, that notorious fish farm attendant that gets its energy for living, not by oxidising its food, but by reducing organic sulphurous compounds. Many readers will have seen what looks like an oil film on bog water and puddles in peatland. It's not oil, but the same iron sulphide (ultimately iron oxide = rust when it comes into contact with the air) manufactured by anaerobic bog bacteria using the same chemical process.

There is much wriggling of tiny *Capitella* worms living in the *Beggiatoa* mat, which are detritivores; i.e. they eat fish farm detritus[131] and other bacteria that enjoy the same diet.

The sea bed in Scottish lochs is usually a riot of biodiversity, which under fish farms gets reduced to a bacterial mat full of little worms. This is known to the industry by the term applied to it by the regulatory authority SEPA ... the AZE, which is the acronym for **A**llowable **Z**one of **E**ffect. Our noble defenders of the environment have defined an area of seabed where ecological destruction (no less) is – according to their standards – allowable.

---

131 Detritus: debris, waste, waste matter, discarded matter, refuse, rubbish, litter, scrap, flotsam and jetsam, lumber, rubble, wreckage.

Do we agree? In considering this, let us particularly bear in mind that aquaculture need not have this appalling detrimental effect on its local environment if sewage dumping not allowed for any other industry were similarly disallowed on fish farms: closed containment (see Chapter 8).

Until instructed to contain fish farm effluent the industry will be delighted that they allowed to pollute (entirely) the region directly beneath fish farms and to some distance beyond as long as SEPA allows them their AZE. As already discussed, the extent to which pollution actually has an effect, though predicted by modelling, is – in biological terms – not properly known at all.

After fish farms have been installed, SEPA monitoring is supposed to ensure that organic sediments and residues of chemical therapeutants, and their ecological consequences are confined that known (predicted) area of sea bed (AZE). That such a region can be defined and its cause known acknowledges that waste discharges from approximately 1,800 salmon cages in Scottish waters do really have detrimental impacts on the sea bed beneath and to some distance beyond the farm itself.

Having a Look At The Sea Bed

You can see what the sea bed beneath a fish farm looks like in several YouTube videos. One which particularly shocked us was *Alex's Migration Meets Fish Farms in Wild Salmon Narrows'* filmed in Canada.[132] References to others are listed below in the same footnote.

> Tavish Campbell (TC): We have an underwater camera here and we're just going to throw it down. We're kind-of in a controlled site here, so it's a clean area, away from the fish farm and we're going to throw it down and see what the bottom [sea bed] looks like.
>
> *An underwater camera attached to a sledge (ROV = Remotely Operated underwater Vehicle) is carefully lowered over the side of the boat into the water. The sea bed survey was instigated and the ROV deployed by local people. We watch the ROV's progress on a monitor screen. The sea bed is composed of reef-forming sea life a diversity of other animals.*
>
> Onboard biologist #1 (OB#1): It's a really neat habitat. Look at all the scallops!
>
> Onboard biologist #2 (OB#2): Yes, you've got squat lobsters, squat prawn ...
>
> OB#1: Big sunstar!
>
> OB#2: Lots and lots of mussels, regular stars, flat stars ...
>
> OB#1: This is just a fabulous habitat, isn't it? All kinds of stuff down there. This is what I talked to you about how it should look like. It's just full of

132 Alex's Migration, from 5 min. 37 sec. https://www.youtube.com/watch?v=MyI3TJ-FjSM
Also see:
https://www.youtube.com/watch?v=vDAT4MK-sNo; https://www.youtube.com/watch?v=eHsOBQgmFnk; https://www.youtube.com/watch?v=nAIShIjPbIE

stuff. The squat lobsters sitting back in the holes, taking off as the camera gets close.

The onboard camera turns to show TC who just grins, fascinated.

TC hauls the ROV aboard and the boat zooms off to another place, where a fish farm can be seen in the background. The next sea bed footage is filmed some distance away from a fish farm (beyond the limits of a Scottish AZE), not beneath it where the camera would probably have shown a mat of Beggiatoa, *apparently lifeless or seething with worms.*

TC: OK, so now we're at the [inaudible name of] farm. We're going to throw the camera down. We just checked out the control site a little ways down the channel. So ... the camera really is our eyes to the bottom down there – what's going on – so we're going to see what it looks like.

Again, we watch the ROV's progress on a monitor screen. Here, the seabed is flat and featureless, apart from a few lifeless objects lying about on the sediment surface.

OB#1: It looks pretty close to dead, doesn't it? We're not seeing much except a whole lot of just sediment down here. This is not a healthy bottom; not a bottom you'd like to see in British Columbia. It's pretty much just sediments with just a few dead shells. It's remarkable by its lack of life. It's very close to a desert but it's a man-made desert – a pretty sad sight. The contrast between this area and the control area further up the channel couldn't be much more striking, could it?

We have spoken to a diver, working at the time on a marine construction project, who had also dived under Scottish salmon farms. What he described matches the lifeless sea bed gunge these videos portray. Allowable Zone of Effect indeed! *Effect*, for goodness' sake! *Extinction*, more like! AZE is a feeble, misleading euphemism intended to ensure that we all underestimate this submarine wasteland of death and destruction. I think we might justifiably rename SEPA's supine[133] AZE as ZAE.

ZAE: Zone of Allowed[134] Extinction

Environmental Impact Assessment

Before any development requiring planning consent may proceed, its potential impact on the environment must be assessed. An Environmental Impact Assessment (EIA) must be carried out and a report (sometimes known as an EIA, sometimes an Environment Statement) delivered to the planning authority.

Well, of course, I hear you say. You would be amazed to see how badly the aquaculture industry complies with this requirement, how slack are the regulators' rules and criticisms and how easily a lousy EIA gets past the scrutineers at the planning office (see Chapters 4 & 10).

---

133 Weak, spineless, yielding, enervated, effete.

134 'Allowable' implies that everybody agrees it's all right. 'Allowed' means that only SEPA might be of the opinion that it's allowable.

There are several excellent hefty documents advising planning applicants how to conduct their EIA. The Crown Estate published a good one a few years ago *Environmental Assessment Guidance Manual For Marine Salmon Farmers*; The Scottish Aquaculture Research Forum (along with our planning authority The Highland Council) has published *Environmental Impact Assessment Practical Guidelines Toolkit For Marine Fish Farming*;[135] and SNH provides a third, possibly the most useful, because it is comprehensive and updated every few years.[136]

> "The EIA process is intended to improve environmental protection. It informs the decision making processes by which public bodies, referred to as 'competent authorities', determine whether certain projects should go ahead. It provides these bodies with a written statement about the project's effects on the environment that are likely to be significant (the environmental statement or 'ES'), together with the comments of the public and statutory environmental organisations." – Scottish Natural Heritage
> *A handbook on Environmental Impact Assessment*

There is no excuse for applicants wishing to install fish farms to get the EIA wrong, but they do so anyway. I expect they see no need to spend any more than a minimum of time and money if the regulators allow them to pollute more-or-less freely and their applications will be waved through anyway because the government is encouraging them to farm lots of fish and not have to bother too much about trivia like the environmental damage they are likely to cause.

Since we, the public, can examine the EIA documents that accompany fish farm planning applications at the same time referring to these highly available documents online or at leisure by downloading and/or printing them, we can at least point out the deficiencies in EIA research and reporting, even though at present the authorities are likely to overlook our criticisms.

The Precautionary Principle

> "Conserving Scotland's marine environment is not just desirable – it is essential to ensure our seas remain healthy and productive into the future."
>
> – MS, SNH & JNCC[137]

3-14 June 1992 saw the United Nations' Earth Summit in Rio de Janeiro. This should have been a turning point for conservation and sustainable development around the world because, at that conference the Precautionary Principle was identified and devised.

The Rio Declaration on Environment and Development was promulgated, twenty-seven principles designed to protect the environment whilst permitting sensible development. Britain was a signatory on that declaration.

---

135 http://www.sarf.org.uk/Project%20Final%20Reports/SARF024%20-%20Final%20Reports%20and%20Templates/EIA%20Guidelines%20FINAL+%20Templates.pdf
136 http://www.snh.gov.uk/docs/A1198363.pdf
137 Large poster produced jointly by Marine Scotland, Scottish Natural Heritage and the Joint Nature Conservation Committee seen in the entrance to SNH headquarters, Inverness.

> Principle 15 states: "Principle 15. In order to protect the environment, the precautionary approach shall be widely applied by States according to their capabilities. Where there are threats of serious or irreversible damage, lack of full scientific certainty shall not be used as a reason for postponing cost-effective measures to prevent environmental degradation." – Rio Declaration, 1992[138]

There is just one little term that seems to give the developer more leeway than nature, *cost-effective*, which seems to be a get-out clause meaning that if you claim you can't afford to conserve, then please carry on regardless. Other than that, it's straightforward: if you don't know what wildlife the place you wish to exploit contains, then you must find out and put mitigation measures in place *before* development may begin. Hence the need for the EIA.

> Principle 17 covers that: "Principle 17. Environmental impact assessment, as a national instrument, shall be undertaken for proposed activities that are likely to have a significant adverse impact on the environment and are subject to a decision of a competent national authority." – Rio Declaration, 1992[139]

That would seem to be straightforward enough and should need no interpretation or elaboration. An EIA has to be carried out and if the developer needs any advice on how to do it and do it right, the documents mentioned above will guide him/her.

You would think that developers and planners would be aware of this and that the former would do the job properly while the latter would oblige him/her so to do.

Sorry. They need to be reminded, and we must keep doing that. It was encouraging to see that, though in first public consultation on a fish farm application that the Sleat community (south Isle of Skye) tackled The Precautionary Principle hardly got a mention, in the second consultation the word had got evidently around. Many people took the opportunity to remind the planners of their obligation to implement The Precautionary Principle.

Also, during the period between application #1 and application #2, the Scottish Government was engaged on creating Marine Protected Areas and, possibly due to our encouraging SNH to consider including the South Skye sea lochs, they carried out a comprehensive and – it should be acknowledged – very competent sea bed survey in Lochs Slapin and Eishort (currently targeted by Hjaltland for three fish farm sites). That survey will no doubt contribute to future planning decisions ... assuming they are considered as we fervently wish them to be, according to Principle 15 of the Rio Declaration.

Everybody, please keep pointing out to the planners that the UK signed the Rio Declaration and that it includes instructions on what to do before development proceeds at any ecologically sensitive site. Whether Scotland will still be part of the UK after 18 September 2014, and whether Scotland will then still be a Rio signatory who recognises The Precautionary Principle, who knows?

---

138 http://www.unep.org/Documents.Multilingual/Default.asp?DocumentID=78&ArticleID=1163
139 Ibid.

Highland Nature & Fish Farms

Highland sea lochs are preferred by salmon farming companies because, among other considerations they could tell readers about: 1. They are the natural habitat of Atlantic salmon *Salmo salar*; 2. The waters are relatively unpolluted ('pristine', I believe they say); 3. Tides and currents help to dilute and disperse salmon faecal and other effluent matter. It is the natural qualities of Scottish sea lochs – which are still relatively unspoilt – that concern those of us who object to net-cage fish farms here.

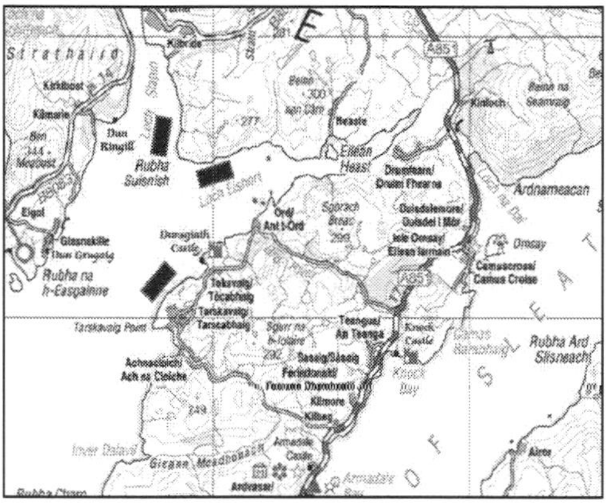

Since this book has been written to help inform communities around the south Skye lochs, we will consider lochs Slapin and Eishort, which are currently being targeted by Hjaltland Sea Farms who are applying for planning permission to install three massive salmon farms there – black rectangles on the map.

Biologists who like me are privileged to live nearby are often to be found exploring the shores of these lochs at low tide. After many years visiting the entire Highland coastline, we reckon the south Skye lochs to be among the best for seashore biodiversity anywhere in Scotland. Unfortunately, walking the shoreline – wonderful though it is – does not allow us to see what is below the waves and we get a mere glimpse of these lochs' natural treasures when examining their margins.

Divers can find a lot more and some have reported some amazing discoveries, particularly after they have visited the sea bed close to the islands the scallop dredgers dare not approach. Where the dredgers have been, the sea bed is at best a ravaged jumble and at worst (and some areas are horribly 'worst') a desert. So aquaculture is not the only threat to biodiversity in these waters.

We know there are instances of the rare habitat founded on the calcareous red alga known locally as 'maerl' (and incorrectly as 'coral', which are colonial animals). Under water this knobbly red seaweed (in these lochs *Phymatolithon calcareum*) forms deep beds riddled with cavities in which a host of other species live. It is an important suite of habitats in itself. When alive it is rich red-purple and when dead it washes up the shore to form stunning white gravel beaches, particularly around the islands between Ord and Borreraig. It is within the vicinity of maerl that we tend to find rarities such as Montagu's, Risso's and hairy crabs, huge purple heart urchins and the rock goby. Common species tend to be more diverse and more numerous here than elsewhere, so for the seashore biologist, the south Skye loch shores are paradise!

During early summer 2014 a team of scientists from SNH carried out a survey of the lochs as part of their investigations in preparation for the designation of new Marine Protected Areas. They travelled in a fast rigid inflatable boat and deployed an underwater camera, methodically examining the sea bed throughout the loch system. What they discovered about maerl distribution surprised us all. We knew it was around Tarskavaig (not far from the southernmost proposed fish farm) and between Ord and

Borreraig (close to the midway proposed fish farm), but we had no idea there was a bed a few hundred metres north of the Loch Slapin proposed fish farm as well as all down the western side of the loch from north of Kilmarie to beyond Glasnakille.

Should the proximity of maerl beds concern the planners when making their decision whether or not to pass applications for fish farms in the south Skye lochs? From the biologist's point of view: I should say so. There is a wealth of scientific literature showing that fish farms are highly detrimental to the maerl habitat, notably through stifling by sedimentation and by eutrophication to both of which maerl is very sensitive. [These detrimental pollution effects have been discussed above.] What the literature has to say about maerl and fish farms will follow shortly, but it vitally important to consider three additional points.

1. **The scientific literature contains much** that shows fish farms have harmful effects on marine ecosystems (habitats), particularly maerl, which has received a disproportionate amount of attention (below). We need to know more about, particularly, the burrowed mud habitat which usually coincides with fish farm development.
2. **There is NO scientific literature whatsoever** that suggests fish farms are anything other than detrimental to marine ecosystems.
3. The south Skye lochs are known to contain several JNCC[140] defined Biodiversity Action Plan (BAP) Priority Habitats[141] and there are indications of a couple of others that require confirmation and, consequently, protection from industrial activities that might be detrimental to them.

The sea bed where two, maybe all, of the proposed fish farms are due to be located has been designated by JNCC as a BAP Priority Habitat identified as *Circumlittoral Muds with Sea Pens & other Megafauna* [SS.SMu.CFiMu.SpnMeg] and by SNH a Priority Marine Feature. This particular habitat is almost entirely restricted to the west coast of Scotland where almost every example has a net-cage fish-farm installed above it. Compare the two maps below, showing fish-farm distribution, left[142] and UK distribution of the burrowed mud habitat, right.[143]

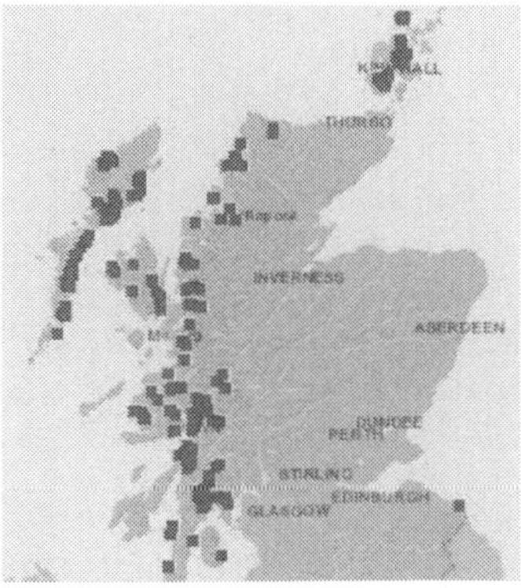

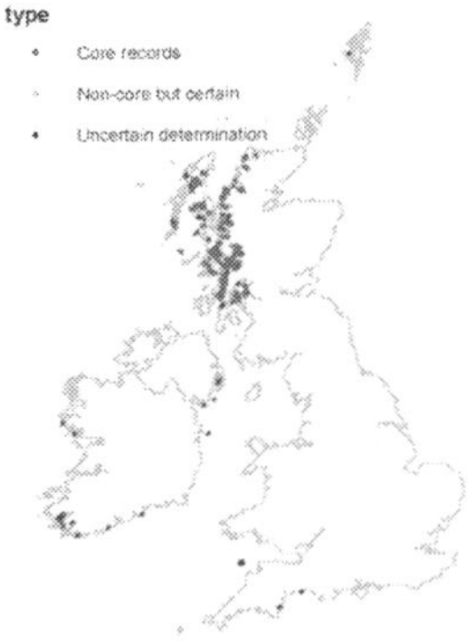

140 Joint Nature Conservation Committee. http://jncc.defra.gov.uk JNCC is a statutory adviser to UK Government and devolved administrations.
141 Internet exploration of Priority Habitats begins here: http://jncc.defra.gov.uk/default.aspx?page=1529
142 Scottish Government, 2013. http://aquaculture.scotland.gov.uk/map/map.aspx
143 JNCC, undated. http://www.jncc.gov.uk/marine/biotopes/biotope.aspx?biotope=JNCCMNCR00001218

The west Scotland localisation of the habitat is clear, as is the striking coincidence with fish-farms. It is acknowledged that a fish-farm does not cover an entire patch of the habitat, but what effect can a fish-farm have over a wide area, and what is the cumulative effect of fish-farms on, perhaps, every example (or most) of a Priority Habitat? I contend that nobody knows and that until research has been carried out, the Precautionary Principle must be implemented.

The south Skye loch system consists of at least four important habitats:

Circumlittoral Muds with Sea Pens & other Megafauna [SS.SMu.CFiMu.SpnMeg]
Circumlittoral Rock and Boulders [LR.MLR.BF.Fser.Bo & IR.MIR.KR.Ldig.Bo]
Maerl Beds [SS.SMp.Mrl]
Sea Grass Beds (*Zostera marina*) [LS.LMp.LSgr]

Divers have reported what are probably file shell nests in the maerl near the Borreraig islands – *File Shell Reefs* (*Limaria hians*) [SS.SMX.IMX.Lim] – a possible fifth special habitat; and if a sixth habitat – *Horse Mussel Reefs* (*Modiolus modiolus*) [SS.SBR.SMus.ModT/Mx/HAs/Cvar] – is not found soon, we will be surprised.

The south Skye loch system has exceptional water quality and noteworthy biodiversity at all levels of ecological importance. There are few places to match it in the whole of Britain and it should be cared for, not squandered on industrial development.

Surely we should heed this unequivocal declaration signed by Marine Scotland, Scottish Natural Heritage and the Joint Nature Conservation Committee:

> "Conserving Scotland's marine environment is not just desirable – it is essential to ensure our seas remain healthy and productive into the future."[144]

Net-cage fish-farms pollute the sea, thus negating the noble aspirations published by the above statutory authorities who represent the Scottish government.

Fish Farms and Maerl: Scientific Literature

Birkett, D.A., C.A. Maggs & M.J. Dring (1998). Maerl (volume V). *An overview of dynamic and sensitivity characteristics for conservation management of marine SACs*. Scottish Association for Marine Science. (UK Marine SACs Project).[145]

> "The positioning of cages over a maerl biotope is likely to lead to fish faeces and partly consumed food pellets contaminating the maerl bed and resulting in anaerobiosis due to the oxygen demand of the decomposing material. The detrital rain from the cages could act in a similar way to terrigenous silt, reducing light penetration through the water column and smothering the maerl surface so that the stabilizing epiphytic algae could no longer establish themselves. As a minimum impact the increase in nutrient levels might produce local eutrophication effects."

---

144 A massive poster seen in the entrance hall of SNH headquarters, Inverness.
145 http://www.ukmarinesac.org.uk/pdfs/maerl.pdf

Grall, J. & J.M. Hall-Spencer (2003). Problems facing maerl conservation in Brittany. *Aquatic Conservation: Marine & Freshwater Ecosystems*. 13: S55-S64.[146]

> "Other major impacts on local maerl bed habitats include the spread of the invasive gastropod Crepidula fornicata, industrial and urban sewage, aquaculture and demersal fishing. These impacts have increased sharply since the 1970s and are causing widespread damage to Breton maerl beds.
>
> "Such declines in one of the most diverse habitats of European waters (BIOMAERL, 1999) have not previously been reported and emphasize the urgent need for maerl bed conservation in France and Europe. The west coasts of Norway, Scotland and Ireland provide similar 'hot-spots' for maerl (Birkett et al., 1998; BIOMAERL, 1999) where active conservation policies are essential if the Breton experience is to be avoided."

Hall-Spencer, J., N. White, E. Gillespie, K. Gillham & A. Foggo (2006). Impact of fish farms on maerl beds in strongly tidal areas. Marine Ecology-Progress. 326: 1-9. Grall J, Hall-Spencer JM (2003). Problems facing maerl conservation in Brittany. *Aquatic Conservation: Marine Freshwater Ecosystems*. 13:55-64.[147]

> "Visible waste was noted up to 100 m from cage edges, and all 3 farms caused significant reductions in live maerl cover, upon which this habitat depends. Near-cage infaunal samples showed significant reductions in biodiversity, with small Crustacea (ostracods, isopods, tanaids and cumaceans) being particularly impoverished in the vicinity of cages, and significant increases in the abundance of species tolerant of organic enrichment (e.g. *Capitella* spp. complex, *Ophryotrocha hartmanni*). Relocation of fish farms to areas with strong currents is unlikely to prevent detrimental effects to the structure and organisation of the benthos, and 'fallowing' (whereby sites are left unstocked for a period of time to allow benthic recovery) is inadvisable where slow-growing biogenic habitats such as maerl are concerned, as this may expand the area impacted."

Haskoning UK Ltd. (2006). Investigation into the impact of marine fish farm depositions on maerl beds. *SNH/SEPA/Marine Harvest Commissioned Report No. 213.*[148]

> "All three fish farm sites had a significant build-up of feed and faeces trapped within maerl near the cages. Evidence of gross organic enrichment was recorded up to 100m away from the cage edges. The organic enrichment was found to affect a number of different aspects of the benthic community.
>
> "Deposition from the fish farms affected the percentage of maerl on the seabed that was live versus dead. All three sites had more dead/dying maerl near to the cages than at the reference sites and at stations distant from the cages. Live maerl close to cage edges had a mottled, unhealthy appearance due to phycobilin pigment loss.

---

146 http://www.ukmpas.org/pdf/Grall_Hall-Spencer_2003.pdf
147 http://www.int-res.com/articles/feature/m326p001.pdf
148 http://www.snh.org.uk/pdfs/publications/commissioned_reports/reportno213.pdf

"Marked reductions in species diversity of infaunal communities associated with the maerl were recorded around the fish farms in Shetland and Orkney. Organic enrichment effects on community structure were also noted around the fish farms in Shetland and South Uist.

"... maerl fragments are often transported in and out of areas of the seabed during storm events. Thus "impacted" maerl fragments close to a fish farm may be transported by waves to a nonimpacted area of seabed. The effect of this is essentially to increase the area of seabed affected by the fish farm."

Hall-Spencer, J. & R. Bamber (2007). Effects of salmon farming on benthic crustaceans. *Ciencias Marinas.* 33(4): 353-336.[149]

"... this study confirmed that maerl habitats are highly susceptible to the effects of fish-farm deposition (possibly compounded by the effects of lice treatment toxicity), showing significant disturbances to the associated crustacean fauna. High organic loading results in the long-term loss of living maerl, upon which formation of the [maerl] habitat depends, and many species are intolerant of smothering by inorganic particulates."

Sanz-Lázaro, C., M.D. Belando, L. Marín-Guirao, F. Navarrete-Mier, A. Marín (2011). Relationship between sedimentation rates and benthic impact on Maërl beds derived from fish farming in the Mediterranean. *Marine Environmental Research.* 71(1): 22–30.[150]

"This work shows that the level of fish farm impact on the benthic community might be underestimated if it is assessed by only taking into account data obtained from waste dispersion rates. The unattached coralline algae habitat studied [maerl] seems to be very sensitive to fish farming compared with other unvegetated benthic habitats."

The Scottish Government, Scotland's Marine Atlas, Inshore and Shelf Subtidal Sediments, Priority Marine Features.[151]

"Maerl beds are extremely sensitive to physical disturbance and smothering, as a result of scallop dredging, bottom trawling, aquaculture and extraction as a fertiliser."

European Community Directive on the Conservation of Natural Habitats and of Wild Fauna and Flora (92/43/EEC).[152]

"... evidence suggests that maerl continues to be under threat from damaging human activities, such as fisheries and fish farm operations. Eutrophication is also considered to be an important threat to maerl beds.

---

149 http://redalyc.uaemex.mx/src/inicio/ArtPdfRed.jsp?iCve=48033403
150 http://www.researchgate.net/publication/47532981_Relationship_between_sedimentation_rates_and_benthic_impact_on_Marl_beds_derived_from_fish_farming_in_the_Mediterranean
151 http://www.scotland.gov.uk/Publications/2011/03/16182005/48
152 http://jncc.defra.gov.uk/pdf/Article17/FCS2007-S1377-audit-Final.pdf

> "The positioning of [fish farm] cages over a maerl bed is likely to lead to fish faeces and partly consumed food pellets contaminating the maerl bed and resulting in anaerobiosis (due to the oxygen demand of the decomposing material). The detrital rain from cages could act in a similar way to terrigenous [land-derived] silt, reducing light penetration through the water column and smothering the maerl surface so that the stabilizing epiphytic algae could no longer establish themselves. As a minimum impact the increase in nutrient levels might produce local eutrophication effects. Indeed, Maggs and Guiry (1987a) noted that maerl below fish cages was covered with *Beggiatoa* sp., which had a detrimental impact on this habitat.
>
> "Hall-Spencer *et al.* (2006) have demonstrated the impacts of Scottish salmon fish farms on maerl and revealed significant reductions in live maerl cover. Indeed visible waste was noted up to 100 m from cage edges and near-cage infaunal samples showed significant reductions in biodiversity, with small Crustacea being particularly impoverished in the vicinity of the cages and significant increases in the abundance of species tolerant of organic enrichment. Maerl is particularly sensitive to hydrogen sulphide, as that generated by fish farm waste (Wilson *et al.* 2004)."

Greathead, G., E. Guirey & B. Rabe (2012). Development of a GIS Based Aquaculture Decision Support Tool (ADST) to Determine the Potential Benthic Impacts Associated with the Expansion of Salmon farming in Scottish Sea Lochs. *Scottish Marine and Freshwater Science* Vol 3 No 6.[153]

> "Within sea lochs there are varying proportions of Priority Marine Features (PMFs), such as Maerl beds that are particularly sensitive to sedimentation and organic enrichment (Hall-Spencer *et al.*, 2006)."

UK Marine SACs Project (2001)

> "Fish farms The positioning of cages over a maerl biotope is likely to lead to fish faeces and partly consumed food pellets contaminating the maerl bed and resulting in anaerobiosis due to the oxygen demand of the decomposing material. The detrital rain from the cages could act in a similar way to terrigenous silt, reducing light penetration through the water column and smothering the maerl surface so that the stabilizing epiphytic algae could no longer establish themselves. As a minimum impact the increase in nutrient levels might produce local eutrophication effects."[154]

Coda of the Pollution Chapter

Business as usual suits the aquaculture industry very well. As far as they are concerned, the environment will have to take it on the chin: "Oh, it'll be OK. Nature will take care of it." How often have we humans put our planet under pressure –

153 http://www.scotland.gov.uk/Resource/0040/00405906.pdf
154 http://www.ukmarinesac.org.uk/communities/maerl/m6_1.htm

atmospheric PCBs and the ozone layer; atmospheric CO_2 and climate change; leaks of radioactivity from badly run power stations; oil spills in seas all around the world; acid generating gases and acid rain; dieldrin, aldrin and lindane of the past and neonicotinoids of today and collateral genocide of bees and other vital creatures; clear-felled rain forests; lifeless, overworked, fertiliser-overloaded soils – for the sake of our convenience, and later discovered we were mistaken about nature's resilience?

If the salmon aquaculture industry were ordered to change (let's say, by a surprisingly yet welcome newly enlightened Scottish Government) they would probably need to downsize and they wouldn't like that. However, a bit of innovative R&D and they might be able to modify existing closed containment systems up to the scale to which they are accustomed, so there ought to be hope for them. Actually getting down to some innovation generating R&D (as opposed to their customary inertia) would cost them money and new equipment would also cost them a lot of money. They *have* a lot of money, and anyway ...

Who should have to pay for the disposal of tonnes and tonnes and tonnes of fish farm effluent: those who stand to make a profit from salmon farming, those who wish to eat cheap farmed salmon or NATURE?

KEY to the McTynn Family and Friends

Emma McTynn – Emamectin Benzoate is an avermectin therapeutant sold as SLICE® for the control of sea lice.

Ivor McTynn – Ivamectin is an avermectin therapeutant chemically related to Emamectin, used in the control of parasites of cattle, mostly as a nematode vermicide.

The Ceilidhsides – Calicide® is the trade name of Teflubenzuron, a growth regulator that prevents moulting in crustaceans, thus controlling sea lice.

Della Methrin – Deltamethrin and Cypermethrin are a pyrethroids used in sea louse control. Deltamethrin is the active ingredient in Alphamax®.

Sally Mosan – Salmosan® is the trade name of a formulation of the organophosphate azamethiphos (said to be less nasty than Dichlorvos).

Richard Lorvoss (a cross-dresser AKA Diana Klorvoss) – Dichlorvos is an organophosphate (very nasty compounds) previously used in the control of sea lice.

Max (Emma's fiancé) – Alphamax® is the trade name of a sea louse control pesticide containing Deltamethrin.

Chapter 7

GOVERNMENT POLICY

The Conflict of Economy *versus* Environment

> "The economy is a wholly owned subsidiary of the environment, not the other way around." – Gaylord Nelson[155]

The Scottish Government holds itself responsible (n.b. on our behalf) for the regulation of Scotland's economic interests while, at the same time, protecting Scotland's environment. These are two aspects of Scotland that must be very difficult to reconcile, for one impinges on the other, not always advantageously.

To put it in more straightforward terms, if you are a mere voter it is impossible to comprehend how the Government can create mutually contradictory policies and carry on as though there are no conflicts. Unless you care more about cash than nature or you underestimate these conflicts out of ignorance (wilfully or not), net-cage salmon farms that leak all their effluent into the sea and the marine environment are not compatible. Neither are policies that fail to recognise this.

Which is the more important, economy or environment? Which should take precedence? American politician (Democrat) and environmental activist Gaylord Nelson put it most succinctly in the aphorism quoted above. If we are to survive, we must consider the place we live before increase in wealth. Many do not agree or find it too inconvenient to acknowledge.

This is not the place to embark upon an extensive argument about economy *versus* ecology. Those of us who consider net-cage fish farming to be a threat to the marine environment clearly take the same side as Gaylord, so let's leave it there and discover the Scottish Government's stance.

It is two-fold – divided – split. The left hand does not involve itself in the doings of the right hand, or if it does (as sometimes it does), the result tends to be equivocal, contradictory or meaningless. There is a distinct lack of joined-up thinking in the economy-environment department of government in which the departments are separate and non-communicating. This is easily illustrated by comparing what the politicians and their agencies state in public.

> "It's great news for Scottish aquaculture. It's great news for the salmon industry. [Farmed] Salmon is part of the essence of Scotland. Two years ago Scots]farmed] salmon sales [to China] were zero. Now they're about fifty million pounds. That's all happened through the work of the [aquaculture] industry and through the work of the Scottish Government, making sure that that great Scottish product is moving into new market places."
>
> – Alex Salmond (Scottish First Minister)

155 Nelson, Gaylord (2002). Beyond Earth Day: Fulfilling the Promise. Wisconsin Press.

"Scotland's seas provide rich and diverse ecosystems that are home to a wide array of plants and animals, including internationally important species. It's our duty to protect this precious environment." – Richard Lochhead, Cabinet Secretary for Rural Affairs and the Environment[156]

"Conserving Scotland's marine environment is not just desirable – it is essential to ensure our seas remain healthy and productive into the future."

– Marine Scotland, Scottish Natural Heritage& JNCC[157]

"The Scottish Government supports Scotland's aquaculture industry to achieve sustainable growth targets, with due regard to the marine environment, by 2020." – The Scottish Government[158]

"Marine Scotland is committed to a clean, healthy, safe, productive and biologically diverse marine and coastal environment that meets the long term needs of people and nature. This includes managing our seas sustainably to protect their rich biological diversity and to ensure that our marine ecosystems continue to provide economic, social and wider benefits for people, industry and society." – The Scottish Government[159]

"Scottish salmon is a high quality, delicious product that is becoming increasingly popular around the world - as illustrated by the latest booming export figures. Last year salmon accounted for 36 per cent of the value of Scottish food exports, while the industry also provides much needed employment opportunities in our fragile rural communities.

"It's important that we continue to promote this key product and encourage further investment in the industry, as well as working with others internationally on ways to continue improving the environmental sustainability of aquaculture. These are areas I will be discussing with my Norwegian and Chilean counterparts, while also sharing successes Scotland has had in the development of our industry."

– Stewart Stevenson, Environment Minister[160]

Does anybody other than me perceive awkward inconsistencies – clashes of interests – in these and other Government declarations? See what others you can find with the assistance of Messrs Google, Bing etc.

156 http://www.scotland.gov.uk/News/Releases/2012/11/SAC02112012
157 Large poster in the entrance lobby of SNH headquarters, Inverness.
158 http://www.scotland.gov.uk/Topics/marine/Fish-Shellfish
159 http://www.scotland.gov.uk/Topics/marine/marine-environment/Conservationstrategy
160 http://www.scotland.gov.uk/News/Releases/2011/08/16122555

Chapter 8

THE FUTURE OF SALMON FARMING

"Closed containment is a proven, viable technology, and is currently used to raise species such as tilapia, trout and salmon in Canada, the US and China. Whether sited on water or land, closed containment systems can:

- eliminate or significantly reduce water column pollution from feed, feces and chemical waste and contamination of the seabed under farms;
- eliminate escapes from the rearing facility;
- eliminate marine mammal deaths due to interactions with farmed fish and nets;
- eliminate or greatly reduce the risk of disease and parasite transfer to wild salmon; and
- significantly reduce the need for antibiotics and chemical treatments in raising fish."

– Farmed and Dangerous[161]

"Closed containers, including fiberglass, cement tanks, and heavy gage plasticized bags, physically separate fish from the external environment. The container's impermeable barrier prevents the transmission of diseases and parasites. It can eliminate escapes and discharges of wastes into the ocean. Eliminating these problems inevitably improves productivity and profits, but there are other environmental and health benefits, too:

- waste can be treated, virtually eliminating pollution of the marine environment,
- wild fish are protected from diseases and parasites,
- fewer chemicals are required, and
- feed use is reduced, lowering pressure on wild fish used in feed." – Pure Salmon Campaign[162]

"ASF supports the development of land-based closed-containment aquaculture. The closer one examines this technology, the more convincing the case for it being the future of salmon farming. In fact, the first commercial operations have already entered market production" – Atlantic Salmon Federation[163]

---

161 http://www.farmedanddangerous.org/solutions/closed-containment/
162 http://www.puresalmon.org/solutions.html
163 http://www.asf.ca/landbased-aquaculture.html

> "It's generally accepted that closed containment aquaculture has the ability to drastically reduce environmental impacts on the marine environment, but there is still debate whether the technology is adequate for commercial-scale production and if it economically feasible? ... land-based closed containment is technically viable on a commercial scale by designing a system using widely available, off-the-shelf components [and] economically viable, with a capital investment that is reasonable and in-line with new technology, and low operating expenses, resulting in a healthy cash flow that materializes in the early years of the operation." – David Suzuki[164]

10th June 2013 was an important day in my life. I changed my mind radically. In the middle of lunchtime seminar at I presented the Harbor Branch Oceanic Institute[165] (HBOI) in Florida, as I touched on salmon fish farming in western Scotland, I dismissed salmon waste as mere 'effluent'. The audience said nothing, but I sensed certain stiffening in their attitude, perhaps laced with a little polite ridicule (not only of me).

Later I was told that my audience included Dr John Scarpa whose research was into methods of closed containment aquaculture. As he later told me (kindly, but in no uncertain terms), to him fish waste constitutes the *nutrients* that feed his systems and the word effluent is entirely inappropriate as far as he's concerned.

John belongs to a team of at least six top biologists with various specialities co-operates in research to produce the most effective Integrated Multi-Trophic Aquaculture systems (IMTA), producing a suite of edible and clean-up species.

After a trip round the 30-acre HBOI Aquaculture Development Park[166] I was completely convinced that, in closed containment systems, 'nutrients' is quite the correct word for what comes out of fishes' bottoms. All apparent waste from the primary fish tanks moves through the system, stage by stage, feeding a series of organisms that gradually use it up until only clean water remains, converting fish poo into people food of various sorts including other fish, shrimp (prawns to us British), oysters and edible seaweed.

The HBOI IMTA system (aka 'aquaponics' = aquaculture + hydroponics) I witnessed was simple, effective and I would say elegant. At the start there was a tank full of fishes, Pompano[167] in this case, carnivores with feed demands similar to those of salmon, though with a less complicated life cycle, so more amenable to farming. Feed pellets go into tank #1 but thereafter the system pretty well feeds itself.

Waste from the Pompano tank is transferred to a tank containing thousands of shrimp and from there through filtration technology before once again feeding creatures in tanks, oysters and small sea urchins. From there the almost clean, but still saline water moves out of doors into the Florida sunshine into the next tanks where seaweeds such as sea lettuce *Ulva lactuca* grow vigorously. There is some additional nutritional input at this stage: sunlight.

---

164 http://www.davidsuzuki.org/ (Closed containment is affordable)
165 http://www.fau.edu/hboi/
166 Elegantly explained and illustrated at http://www.fau.edu/hboi/aquaculture/
167 Probably *Trachinotus carolinus*, a mackerel-like fish in the family known as Jacks.

Shown HBOI's indoor contained aquaculture by John completely changed my outlook on fish farming from hopeless/helpless to optimistic/enthusiastic, at least within the practical possibilities. Best of all, I understood why closed tanks and recirculation are preferable to conventional fish pens and polluted seas, and had learnt it from first-hand experience, not just from books or the internet.

A splendid flash of inspiration occurred to me some months later when I realised that the simple word HOLES summarised all that is wrong with open net-cage fish farms. The answer – and it is entirely practical, if costly – is to do away with the holes, keep all the muck in the system, treat it and use everything that can be recycled to make additional food (and profit!).

As soon as I had left HBOI I was itching to tell everybody back home about closed containment aquaculture and, as John had shown me, its associated extension 'aquaponics'. Not only can water from fish rearing tanks be cleaned up for re-use, but nutrients originating in fish feed and emerging as excrement can feed a series of animals and plants that can, like the fish, be consumed by humans. Salmon farming as currently conducted in Scotland with its accompanying pollution problems– if the aquaculture industry would play a fair game, perhaps encouraged by an enlightened government – could be cleaned up and made acceptable to those of us who would prefer the industry did not pollute the sea and get away with it.

I soon learnt that advocates of conventional salmon farming don't argue against closed containment from knowledge and evidence. They simply express contempt for closed containment. They pompously assert that:

1. It has been proven not to work. Untrue. *Please refer to the list of people who are already in production using closed containment.*

2. That it cannot match the scale of production they aspire to. Not quite true. *If they want closed aquaculture on a massive scale they need to tackle the problem – which has almost been solved anyway, with concerted R&D effort. They can afford it.*

3. That it would cost a lot for them to convert now that they are underway with their net-cages. *True, but they could afford to convert and probably would if instructed by the government that they must change their methodologies or cease production altogether. Governments subsidise green energy projects; why not green aquaculture?*

So we need an enlightened government to act on this one. We must send a copy of this book to the environment ministers and then must lobby them persistently until they get the message. Of course, if we can be shown to be wrong about this, we will make a sharp about turn, but considering all the evidence, I don't think that is likely to be necessary.

Closed containment aquaculture is already operating on a commercial scale. Many species of fish are now being reared in tanks with recirculation, not only the easy ones like Carp and Tilapia – even Atlantic salmon! Visit the AKVA Group's website.[168]

168 http://www.akvagroup.com/products/land-based-aquaculture/recirculation-systems

If the aquaculture industry in Scotland complains that contained systems cannot match the scale of production they need, the closed fish farms Octaform say they can build suggest otherwise.[169]

SweetSpring, a closed containment company rearing Coho Salmon in Washington State, U.S.A., is not only in production and has been for several years, they also do not pollute, use no pesticides or medicines, their product is said to have excellent eating quality and they have a particular boast: ranked Super Green by Monterey Aquarium Seafood Watch. *SweetSpring* and wild-caught Alaska Salmon are the only salmon listed as Super Green. No other salmon is considered sustainable by Seafood Watch. I wonder where Seafood Watch would rank Marine Harvest, Hjaltland, Scottish Salmon Company, Scottish Seafarms *et al*?

What are the advantages and disadvantages of closed containment?

NET-CAGE	**CLOSED CONTAINMENT**
Full of holes, open to the sea	No holes, fully contained
Waste disposed of in the sea	Waste contained
Marine environment polluter	No pollution
Waste treatment non-existent, therefore completely free	Waste treatment costs money, but see next two:
Waste is thrown away	Waste is can be reused
Waste is not recycled	Waste can be recycled
Pests & Diseases affect farmed fishes	Pests & Diseases greatly reduced
Pests & Diseases affect wild fishes	Pests & Diseases do not affect wild fishes
Pesticides & Medicines required	Pesticides & Medicines much reduced
Pesticides & Medicines pollute	Pesticides & Medicines do not pollute
Fishes escape	Fishes do not escape
Genetic contamination of wild fishes	No genetic contamination of wild fishes
Invasion by carnivorous mammals and birds	Carnivorous mammals and birds excluded
Carnivorous mammals and birds 'culled'	Carnivorous mammals and birds excluded
Cages damaged or destroyed by rough seas	Cages not damaged by rough seas
Creates a few new jobs	Creates a few new jobs
Contribution to local economy?	Contribution to local economy?
Fish feed contains wild caught fish as meal	Fish feed contains wild caught fish as meal

169 http://www.octaform.com/applications/aquaculture/

If we need convincing that there contained aquaculture has something to contribute a journey around YouTube pursuing search terms such as “closed containment” and “aquaponics” is most enlightening. We find instruction by enthusiasts rearing a wide variety of fish (including salmon) at all scales of production on household roofs and balconies; in backyards and greenhouses; in community initiatives; on conventional farms whose owners are diversifying; and in extensive industrial installations. Many people are also growing fruit and vegetables in hydroponic culture, plumbed into their fish farms so as to take advantage of the nutrients their fish containers provide.

Contained aquaculture and aquaponics are in production all around the world, yet the advocates for conventional fish farming lead us to believe that closed containment is ‘unproven’ or ‘impractical’.

That is arrant nonsense.

We, the public, must not waste any opportunity when voicing our opposition to net-cage salmon farming to remind the authorities that workable alternatives that do not pollute the marine environment are possible and, in fact, are already available. We must point out that closed containment aquaculture can be conducted anywhere and is best situated, not in remote regions such as the West Highlands (though in that region we will find the conversation diverted into an argument about employment, so a case for that needs to be prepared in advance) but close to the customer, perhaps using brown field sites that are crying out for development. Fish farms could even be constructed alongside motorways, where transport access would be a lot more convenient than in the Highlands, or adjacent to railways, which would make transport cheap and keep CO_2 emissions down.

The Problem, as the table shows, is that net-cage fish farming as currently conducted has many disadvantages.

The Solution is that they can all be eliminated by adopting closed containment aquaculture.

Closed containment aquaculture is, as they say, a no-brainer!

Who has something to say about closed containment for rearing farmed salmon?

Kuterra Land-Based Closed Containment Salmon Farm
http://www.namgis.bc.ca/CCP/Pages/default.aspx

Hydronov Deep Water Hydroponic Growing Technology
http://www.hydronov.com/

Octaform The Best Recirculating Aquaculture Systems In The World
http://www.octaform.com/applications/aquaculture/

Sweet Spring Salmon
http://sweetspringsalmon.com/

Living Oceans
http://www.livingoceans.org/initiatives/salmon-farming

AKVA Group Aquaculture
http://www.akvagroup.com/products/land-based-aquaculture/recirculation-systems

Closed Containment Videos

Closed containment - The future of fish farming Living Oceans
https://www.youtube.com/watch?v=qYCEGtMdORU

Freshwater Institute: Closed-Containment Aquaculture Systems
https://www.youtube.com/watch?v=t95KsHOfH0g

Hydronov Deep Water Hydroponic Growing Technology
https://www.youtube.com/watch?v=S1AHtcgXrFM

Kaldnes® RAS, Recirculating Aquaculture System
https://www.youtube.com/watch?v=Umt79lXnNuY

Octaform The Best Recirculating Aquaculture Systems In The World
https://www.youtube.com/watch?v=J1LJAd_oQMA

Chapter 9

FISHES FED TO FISHES

> "Salmon is heavily marketed as one of the healthiest food sources around. But there's an environmental cost. The way it gets its beneficial omega 3 oils is by being fed other oily fish; wild fish such as anchovies, spratts, herring and capelin." – Hugh Fearnley-Whittingstall[170]

The best case against this aspect of fish farming that I've seen was argued in the first series of the Channel 4 TV programme *Hugh's Fish Fight*, screened in 2011.[171] In episode 3 our intrepid investigator Hugh Fearnley-Whittingstall (HF-W) visited a couple of Scottish fish farms, one owned by the world's largest farmed salmon producer Marine Harvest and the other an organic community-run fish farm somewhere in the Shetlands.

He did not concern himself, as I do (Chapters 5 & 6), with the pollution caused by net-cage fish farms – it's as well that we each contribute what we can and are best at to this multi-faceted debate – but concentrated entirely on the fishy ingredient in the pellets fed to farmed salmon. The international lust for salmon to eat requires that millions of salmon get a healthy diet, which as near as it can mimics what they would eat in the wild. Salmon are carnivores and much of what they eat is other fishes.

Salmon do not thrive if not fed at least some nutrients found in fish flesh. They need less than wild fishes because all they do all day is swim languidly round and round, under exercised (therefore, the meat is less 'toothsome' than that of wild-caught salmon – mentioned in Chapter 3). But they have to have some fish in their diet, to obtain the omega 3 fatty acids with which oily wild fishes are richly laced.

Therefore, the feed manufacturers include a certain amount of fish meal and fish oil in their pellet formulations and the source of this material is small oily fishes, hoovered out of the sea, usually on the other side of the planet, and imported. When my colleague Roger and I presented our fish farming show at a hall in Ullapool there was a bit of a stir when one of the fish farm lads present took exception to my referring to trawlers 'hoovering' fishes out of the sea. At the time, I politely apologised (fingers crossed behind my back), though to my mind I was using the word in a light hearted way, not trying to be offensive to anyone. Significantly, I was unaware that what I'd said was more-or-less true.

I later discovered that when the fishing boats that gather huge quantities of these small fishes for processing find a dense shoal they don't deploy a net. Instead they have a flexible tube with a conical device on the end which they put into the sea and then simply suck up the fishes, a procedure that might well be compared with hoovering.

---

170 Hugh's Fish Fight, episode 3. Channel 4 TV, January 2011. See if it's still available where I saw it in 2014 on Channel 4 on demand (4OD). http://www.channel4.com/programmes

171 Also a website http://www.fishfight.net/

Immense tonnages of little fishes that HF-W considers to be as good to eat as salmon, if not better (I agree, being a huge fan of fried sand eels in tempura batter, not to mention whitebait) get squeezed of their oil, then baked and ground into fish meal. These products are then shipped halfway round the world to feed farmed salmon which – assuming we haven't taken a stand never to touch the stuff – we then buy cheaply, overlooking the environmental cost.

The Marine Harvest representative who showed HF-W around their Loch Linnhe fish farm was unable to discover how much of the fish feed they used consisted of wild small fishes, which amazed HF-W who pressed him to come up with an answer:

> HF-W: I'm surprised you don't know that, Steve, because that's one of the key figures in the whole discussion.

At first the rep. completely missed the point and trotted out company dogma ...

> SB: The important thing for us is more on the conversion that we're getting from putting this feed into our fish.

... but the pressure was on ...

> HF-W: The important thing for the environment, surely, is how much wild fish is being killed to produce farmed salmon. We're coming here to talk about the sustainability of your operation and you must have known this was going to be one of my lead questions. I'm surprised you don't have the answer.

To his credit, with his feet held to the fire, the rep. promised, "I'll get that figure", but we weren't told any more during the programme. I tried to find out for myself, searching the internet, but couldn't get hold of any reliable figures. It seems the feed companies are reluctant to publish such information. Anyway, we know that, unless otherwise stated, salmon feed pellets contain a certain proportion of oil and solids obtained from wild small fishes by hoovering them out of the Pacific.

Ah yes, *unless otherwise stated.* There are alternatives to wild small fishes, some successfully employed, some requiring further R&D. From Marine Harvest, HF-W went off to visit a small community-run organic salmon farm somewhere in Shetland. There he was assured that feed pellets used contained no specially caught wild fish. The fishy component was all off-cuts and trimmings from the preparation of fish for human consumption: heads, fins, skeletons, guts etc. Any objections we might have to that would take us into different arguments about fishing and need not concern us here.

Other people are trying quite hard to satisfy farmed salmons' need for fish in their diet by exploiting other sources of the required nutrients, in particular the omega 3 oils. Some are using artificially reared king ragworm *Alitta virens* though I have no idea whether it is a satisfactory alternative or partial alternative to small wild oily fishes. If it is, then I say get on with the worm farming.

I once read in *New Scientist* that a genetically modified plant crop could soon become a supplier of omega 3 that might supply the salmon farm feed industry. That too sounds like a good idea as long as it doesn't cause food shortages by taking over valuable growing land or mean that even more rain forest will be brutally clear felled to make way for biofuel cropping. They who might produce alternatives to wild little oily fishes must keep on the lookout for unforeseen consequences of their actions.

There are other initiatives under test, using mussels and algae to replace small wild fishes, but they have yet to come into production. It would be a great boost they were successful. That would satisfy the only possible objection to closed containment fish farming (Chapter 8). N.B. the problem of wild fish in fish feed pellets applies to all forms of aquaculture that use them.

Finally, I want to quote a few choice lines from the *Hugh's Fish Fight*, taken from his conversation with the representative of Marine Harvest (SB). If such a feeble argument satisfies its originator and persuades the public, then I'm worried. I'm glad Hugh has exposed it and I hope people notice how weak an argument it is.

> HF-W: Does it worry you, the fundamental principle underlying this, [that] you have to kill wild fish to farm farmed salmon? Is that not a fundamental flaw with the entire enterprise?
>
> SB: No, I disagree, because the fish that we're using will be fish that are short-lived fast-growing fish and maybe not that appealing to eat. A lot of people say, "I don't like fish because of the bones." What we can deliver in salmon is fish that is well prepared; it doesn't have any bones and people like that.
>
> HF-W: I think that that's a little bit depressing, to think that the entire reason this operation is happening, the entire reason that you're producing close to three-hundred and fifty tonnes of salmon a year and that's because people don't like small fish with bones. That's the reason for this entire industry, isn't it?
>
> SB: Well, I think people see salmon as available, it's affordable, it tastes good, it's safe – we know what it's been fed on – it's got a lot of attributes that people like. That's the reason that they buy it.
>
> HF-W: Boneless fillets of farmed salmon may be popular with shoppers, but environmentalists are less keen. *Next he mentioned another aspect of his concern about salmon farming.* Besides the issue of feed sustainability, many claim that the stocks of wild salmon are being decimated by parasites that build up on the farms. Sea lice thrive on these densely stocked fish. To reduce fatalities they're regularly dowsed in chemicals that kill the lice. But as lice numbers build up between treatments, the wild salmon that inhabit these waters are easily infested, and they can't be treated.

In the same programme HF-W, Jamie Oliver and other chefs cooked a selection of delicious little fishes in public (I think it must have been on the lawns by the Houses of Parliament) to find out whether people did mind eating such fishes bones and all. It was quite clear that many were delighted. Outside a supermarket, shoppers were challenged – as in a sixties washing powder commercial – to swap the farmed salmon they had just bought for three times the weight of alternative fish, cooked for them to taste there and then. Many of those who tried the alternatives made the swap.

The message was clear: people don't mind the bones and will eat all sorts of fish when it is prepared properly. Thank you Hugh and crew.

Chapter 10
WHAT CAN WE ORDINARY PEOPLE, DO?

"These lochs are your lochs, These lochs are my lochs,
From Shetland, Orkney, Hebrides, From Cape Wrath to Kintyre,
These lochs were made for you and me.
These sea lochs were made for you and me."
– after Woody Guthrie, 1940

The Lerwick Declaration

"We believe that the people who live and work in Scotland are best placed to make decisions about our future – the essence of self-determination; therefore we support subsidiarity and local decision making.

"It follows, therefore, that any government committed to that policy should listen to the views expressed across all of Scotland ..." – First Minister, Alex Salmond MSP, 25 July 2013

Dearbhadh Lerwick

"Tha sinn a' creidsinn gur iad na daoine a tha a' fuireach agus ag obair ann an Alba a tha san t-suidheachadh as fheàrr gus co-dhùnaidhean a dhèanamh mun àm ri teachd againn – brìgh fèin-dhearbhaidh; mar sin tha sinn a' cur taic ri bhith a' toirt cumhachd nas fhaisge air na daoine agus a bhith a' dèanamh cho-dhùnaidhean gu h-ionadail." – Am Prìomh Mhinistear, Ailig Salmond BPA, 25 Iuchar 2013

The Learning Curve

There is a great deal we ordinary folk can do, either to support or object to fish farming, but be warned: contrary to the aspirations expressed by the Alex Salmond's Lerwick Declaration, the authorities have imposed limitations to public involvement in the planning consultation process – discussed below and mentioned in Chapter 1 – which we must resist. At the time of writing we are just becoming aware of what we may and (more to the point) may not do to play a meaningful role in fish farm decision making. That section will be updated as we learn become more familiar with the workings of the planning process. We will also remember to draw any unreasonably obstructive authority's attention to that declaration (and the proposed Community Empowerment and Renewal Bill[172] when it has passed through parliament) when we

172 "The proposed Community Empowerment and Renewal Bill will support communities to achieve their own goals and aspirations through taking independent action and by having their voices heard in the decisions that affect their area." http://www.scotland.gov.uk/Topics/People/engage/cer

encounter officious obstacles that prevent us expressing our well-informed opinions and having them mean something.

I contend that any case, for or against, should stand on a firm foundation of knowledge, which is not easy to assimilate all the way from the point of total ignorance *whence I myself came*. What has struck me as I got up to somewhere approaching 'speed' on the subject was just how little most people know about fish farming, especially all the disadvantages. I often find myself explaining to people why I object to net-cage salmon farms in Scottish sea lochs and as the facts sink in, assuming I am right and they believe me, they rapidly change their own minds, in the same way as I changed mine as of October 2012.

Exposing their ignorance is in no way meant to denigrate other people. The days when a single brain could contain just about all there is to know in the world are several centuries gone. There is more to learn these days than any one of us can ever hope to learn, so of course there are many areas in which we know less than other people and many in which we know pretty well nothing. I won't bore you with a list of all the things I don't know, but I can tell you it's very, very long.

So that's where I was eighteen months ago, utterly and hopelessly ignorant on the subject of aquaculture. Until then I had no idea how profoundly and potentially harmfully ignorant I was! I was happily sailing along through life vaguely of the opinion that if people were farming fish, then that must be stopping them over fishing wild fish, so that must be all right.

vagueness + opinion = not very clever

I ask you to catch up with me on the information accumulation front and I will do my best through this book to share with you what I have found out, to save you the trouble of searching it all yourself. The situation isn't pretty and it is a rather complicated subject, so what I ask of you won't be easy, but I have tried very hard to make what I've written as objective and evidence based as I can. Some of my opinions will have slipped in and I hope readers will weed out any that are no better than mere opinions (or worse, dogma). If I've done a good job, you won't find any.

The learning curve is a steep and treacherously slippery slope, and its component nuggets of understanding won't arrive at your desk in an organised queue; rather they will tend to overlap and sometimes provoke a lot of puzzled head scratching. However, please:

- Learn as much as you can stomach about the aquaculture industry.
- Learn how fish farms are constructed and how they work (Chapter 3).
- Learn as much marine biology/ecology as possible. That's the best bit: going to the seashore to find out what wildlife it has to offer for your enthusiastic fascination, and maybe snorkelling or diving to have a look right under water.
- Learn about the fish farm controversy, pro and con (Chapter 4).
- Search the internet to get answers to questions that will inevitably crop up (and to check that what I've said is correct and true) and watch the relevant YouTube videos, many which I have found very instructive and some thoroughly unconvincing. As always, don't assume that internet stuff you find is true – filter it according to what you know to be true with a generous helping of scepticism and common sense.

- Decide which parts of the controversy (Chapter 4) you feel most comfortable discussing and concentrate on them, setting the others aside until, perhaps, you free up some spare brain space and can have a go at them as well.
- Find and interpret the relevant science through peer-reviewed papers (whilst learning from but not getting informed by bad science, which is common and will attack you from many directions). Don't be scared by the science – persevere.
- There are environmentalists – how I hate the term; how about concerned biologists – who argue a reasoned case and there are idiots who, take one well-known instance, release mink into the wild, thinking they are helping the cause. Gauge opinion from responsible, evidence based, plausible websites, disregarding those that you can tell are over opinionated, lacking in evidence based authority, dangerous or just plain silly.
- Visit places that overlook fish farms and others for which planning is being sought, to see what the land- and seascape looks like before and after installation of a fish farm.
- Follow fish farm planning applications online (see below) and send the planning officers your informed opinions when consultations open. The more informed you become, the stronger and more effective your comments will be, but please don't be put off if you can't keep up with all aspects of the fish farm argument. This subject makes some very hard work when we start from zero, and we can all only do our best. When a public consultation opens, send in your comments of any reasonable standard, because even the number of letters for *versus* against might count. The more often you contribute to a consultation, the better you get at it. Actually, it's possible that the planning officers might have time to consider only relatively trivial indicators like how many objections there are, whilst overlooking detailed, well-informed academic discussion.

Scientific Publications

We are most fortunate that we now have the internet as a source of scientific literature. If you work at a university, the chances are you have a decent library plus free accounts with scientific journals and search facilities. Most of us have to make do, and we can do very well with a bit of clever searching and judicious reading.

We all find that papers on subjects about which we know little can be rather baffling or seem utterly impenetrable. I think the best advice is please don't be put off. If the information seems to be sound and relevant, get what you can from a paper and then lay it aside, somewhere where it can't intimidate you further. Don't hurt your brain unnecessarily.

There are several ways in which reliable scientific information can be obtained online, sometimes with infuriating limitations which we just have to put up with or circumvent in some ingenious way:

1. **Open Access Journals** Some scientific journals publish entire papers online for all to read. That is most generous and a wonderful resource for those of us who can't otherwise get hold of them to read *or* (it's worth always having this self-limiter at the back of your mind) ignore if the information they contain is either irrelevant, incomprehensible or just plain bad.

2. **Subscription Journals** If a search takes you to a journal that requires payment you're not entirely stuck. You can, of course, subscribe or send a one-off payment. However, they always provide the abstract (summary) – which with a bit of luck will tell you what you need to know – plus the full reference, which you must cite so that others may confirm or dispute what you have deduced from the literature you have 'mined'. [Let the fish farm people issue outrageous unsubstantiated assertions (as they do, to the extent that on mature reflection we might justifiably recognise what they say as 'false witness'). As honest citizens, we will make sure that *everything* we say or write is to the best of our knowledge correctly represented and available for confirmation or disputation. That's the way of proper science, which can be trusted.]

   Here's a couple of examples of how a reference might be cited. Different journals have different conventions, but these are fairly standard. The main thing is that it should be entirely identifiable so that anybody else may be able to read it.

   A two-author paper: Merryweather J.W. & Fitter A.H. (1998). The arbuscular mycorrhizal fungi of *Hyacinthoides non-scripta*. II. Seasonal and spatial patterns of AMF populations. *The New Phytologist* 138: 131-142. [In the text cited as (Merryweather & Fitter, 1998)]
   A multi-author paper: Helgason T., Merryweather J.W., Denison J., Wilson P., Young P.J. & Fitter A.H. (2002). Selectivity and functional diversity in arbuscular mycorrhizas of co-occurring fungi and plants from a temperate deciduous woodland. *Journal of Ecology*. 90: 371-384. [In the text cited as (Helgason *et al*., 2002)]
   A book: Merryweather J.W. (2007). *The Fern Guide*. 3rd. edition. Field Studies Council: Shrewsbury (ISBN 978 1 85153 228 5). [In the text cited as (Merryweather, 1998)]
   A web document: Consultee response (SNH) to fish farm planning application, Loch Snizort East (14/0595/FUL) *Here print the URL of the web page.*

3. **Reference Lists** All scientific papers come with a huge list of references to the literature used to inform the research, discuss it in its context and compose the paper. Of course, this literature list will be related to what you are interested in to a greater of lesser degree and can take you to other relevant papers and other long lists of references. You will have to make a lot of painful decisions about which might be useful, needing to be followed up, and which not to bother with. I'm afraid you will often discover that the one paper you can sense might provide the evidence you really need is for some reason frustratingly unobtainable. All you can do is keep trying every strategy you know that might find it until you get lucky or decide to give up.
4. **Authors' Websites** Quite a few academics have a CV on their website and, if you're lucky, their publications list will have links to abstracts, full papers at their publishers' websites or PDFs that are just as useful.
5. **Reprint Request** If you have only a citation of (reference to) a paper, and you can find the first author's contact details, you can request a reprint. If the author has not sent out all copies (the publisher supplies a heap of them for this purpose) they will send you one.
6. **Other Information** An internet search will throw up all manner of information in all sorts of formats, which you will have to assess and sift to get the most relevant

and reliable. Be careful of chat lines and crusade websites, which might contain perfectly valid or wildly inaccurate information. Also take care when dealing with newspaper reports, especially their headlines, which will have been composed to grab readers' attention, not provide scientific data.

7. **Internet Searching** I have discovered there are many ways to get Google to find you what you're looking for. Sometimes you have the title of a paper. Put it all in the search box with inverted commas to tell Google you want it to look just for that title (don't type it wrong – copy & paste if possible). If that fails, try different expressions of the authors' names specific to that paper and then reduce the list until you are left with only the first author's name. Good search engines will even find – if that's what you have – phrases from within a paper, though you might then find that to get into the paper where that phrase is you need to get past a pay wall.
8. **Information Begets Information** As you search two particular things will happen: 1. You will get sidelined by other interesting stuff – your decision what to do next; 2. Related information arises, sometimes several packets at a time so that you lose your original thread. Sorry.
9. **University Friends** If you really need to get hold of a paper and you have a kind friend with a university library or literature account and you are prepared to wait for it to arrive, tell them what you need.
10. **Get Clever** I'm certain I haven't worked out or suggested here all the ways to get the best out of the internet. Good luck.

Send the planners your informed comments in every consultation

Once you have as much information as you can gather it will be time to write your letter of support or objection to the planning application. At the Highland Council we get just one stab at this, so this letter has to hit the spot. I don't know about the others, listed below, but since the process is overseen by the Scottish Government, I doubt they will be very different.

Planning applicants who are not satisfied with the council's decisions have the right of appeal, and if still dissatisfied, may probably take their objections right up to the national government.

I have been informed that we, the public, have no right of appeal whatsoever. Once the council has made its decision, we are expected to accept it. This does not seem to me to be in accord with our noble leader's Lerwick Declaration, the proposed Community Empowerment and Renewal Bill or, indeed, democracy itself.

We in south Skye do not yet have experience of a successful fish farm planning bid, but I suspect that if the council finds in favour of any that do affect us we will not want to take it lying down, as they probably expect us to do. We have already learnt that there are plenty of reasons why fish farm applications currently being processed are inappropriate in the sites proposed and accompanied by documentation of lamentable quality that properly critical planning officers – who are after all our public servants – should find completely unacceptable. There will be no way we will not have something quite insistent to say if the applications that concern us are waved through unopposed.

The Planning Process (fish farms)

Visit the council's planning (or 'eplanning') website. There you can find out which planning applications are at which stage.

Argyll & Bute Council:
http://www.argyll-bute.gov.uk/planning-and-environment
The Highland Council:
http://www.highland.gov.uk/info/161/planning_and_building_standards
Comhairle nan Eilean Siar:
http://www.cne-siar.gov.uk/planningservice/disclaimer.asp?tabindex=1
Shetland Islands Council:
http://www.shetland.gov.uk/planning/
Orkney Islands Council :
http://www.orkney.gov.uk/Service-Directory/D/Development-Management.htm
North Ayrshire Council:
http://www.north-ayrshire.gov.uk/resident/planning-and-building-standards/planning-and-building-standards.aspx
Other Councils:
http://www.scotland.gov.uk/About/Government/councils

Stage 1. Application Not available for public to view until Stage3.

Stage 2. Screening and Scoping A pre-consultation phase during which the applicant fills in forms with preliminary information. Documents are available online, but not yet advertised to the public. A Screening Opinion allows applicants to find out whether a proposal requires an Environmental Impact Assessment (EIA) before making a planning application. Only developments which may have a significant environmental effect require an EIA to be produced. *Absolutely essential with an acknowledged polluting installation such as a fish farm.* If an EIA is required for a development, applicants can seek advice on what needs to be included by requesting a Scoping Opinion.

Stage 3. Pending Consideration The application documents are online and are joined, one-by-one, by responses from all the interested regulatory authorities: SNH, SEPA, Marine Scotland, Crown Estate, Historic Scotland, Transport Scotland and several others. Sometimes these have not all arrived by the time public consultation has begun. Since the application cannot be fully analysed if consultee comments are missing, it is important that we notice such deficiencies and write asking for these documents to become available a.s.a.p. or – they won't like it – demanding an extension of the consultation period.

Stage 4. Public Consultation This will be advertised in the local newspapers (as well as, I think, in Edinburgh) and a closing date given, which in the Highland Council region is a month from the date of the paper. At this point we need to get our skates on, but hopefully we have already done some preparation or might even have our comment letter completed in anticipation.

Stage 5. Decision We have yet to experience a fish farm planning decision. There was a withdrawal, but that doesn't really count, and I can't remember how I found out when it happened – perhaps because of news from friends by e-mail. If, as I am recommending, we are going to appeal against bad decisions – in spite of our having no right to do so! – we need to know as soon as an application decision has been made. *I must find out and update this section.*

Special (slightly sneaky) Advice The Highland Council's eplanning website has a form we can fill in with our details (not to be published) and comments. Press the [Make a Public Comment] button. When I submitted my first ever, quite long and carefully formatted comment letter it turned up on the Public Comments page as a single several-thousand-word paragraph, all formatting completely gone. So, if your comment is brief and simple, that works well and please use the facility. If your letter is complicated, as mine are, why not use this alternative strategy? Write your letter using a conventional word processor and convert it into a PDF to send to the planning office as an attachment with an covering e-mail. After a brief hiatus, it will appear online exactly as you have formatted it, albeit with your address and signature redacted with a great big black splodge, along with any other bits the council considers for-their-eyes-only. Defamatory text, personal e-mail addresses and URLs for campaign websites will also probably get blacked out, so be careful not to be rude about anybody.

Tracking an Application I thought I had set the eplanning website so that I would receive notification of progress with planning applications, but so far I have received none when maybe (says me) I should have. Maybe I filled in the dialogue wrong. Look out for a [Track] button or similar and try it yourself. It is very easy to get left behind by activity on an application, particularly if you're following several at a time, so tracking should be very handy.

Finding the Right Web Pages I have only experience with the Highland Council's eplanning website, so that's what I will describe, hoping yours will be similar.

3. Go to your council's website.
4. Find the planning pages (or search for your council's name+planning).
5. View planning applications.
6. Search for planning applications.
7. Enter key words etc.
8. Select the appropriate application description and go to its pages.
9. View the comments. There are consultee comments and public comments, so if you want to count how many have come in from the public: total minus consultees. Comments submitted using the online form will appear on this page. Comments sent in as PDFs will be listed and can be read by switching to the Documents page.
10. View documents. You will find the application form here plus all supporting documents, the consultees' responses and assorted other documents. This makes fascinating reading if you have time and patience. This is where I have read some appallingly unprofessional documents submitted by fish farm companies saving time and money, thinking they will get away with it. Not any more, if I have anything to do with it. If we are to lose a battle, better if it's against a competent, fair-playing opponent!

This edition of 'HOLES' was produced in a hurry so that the information in it could be laid out before the community of Sleat, Isle of Skye in the run up to public consultation on a brace of planning applications for fish farms to be installed in Loch Eishort (14/02574/FUL & 14/02577/FUL).

At the time of printing we are awaiting the outcome of battles already fought over two applications to put a fish farm at the same Loch Slapin site, off Suisnish, first submitted by Marine Harvest in 2012 (12/03607/FUL) and inexplicably withdrawn at the eleventh hour, then repeated by Hjaltland Seafarms Ltd. in 2014 (14/01467/FUL).

It is intended that after more work a more complete, polished and less geographically specific edition (with its yet to be compiled index) will be published so that other people might know what industrial indignities are being imposed by big business on our once 'pristine' Highland sea lochs.

– James Merryweather, August 2014

Blue-Skye BOOKS

http://www.blue-skye.org.uk

User-Friendly Seashore Guide was prepared to serve the specific needs of the Highland (Scotland) Seashore Biodiversity Project, 2013-2015 and also to present a new, intermediate-grade identification kit suitable for seashore enthusiasts around Britain.

Users are strongly encouraged to avoid picture-matching, a haphazard process that often results in misidentifications, and to work their way through reliable identification keys resembling those used by specialists, but with an innovative twist that contrasts with their scientific counterparts:

So that they can be approached by all users, the keys are couched in plain English and contain virtually no technical terms.

Whilst users need to adopt methodical patience (as opposed to the randomness of picture matching), they should find the stepwise keys highly accessible, painlessly discovering the identities of most common seashore species found around the Highland coast. Further information about more species can be looked up in the more advanced literature.

To be effective, all identification guides must be tested. It is expected that early versions of *User-Friendly Seashore Guide* will require modification and expansion after each occasion when they are used. Publication with Amazon's CreateSpace, in which only the number of copies required are printed to order, means that new versions may be produced as required. The book will improve and expand as the project progresses. After three years of testing and additions, we should be able to publish a thoroughly competent new-look field guide.

PAPERBACK – from Amazon

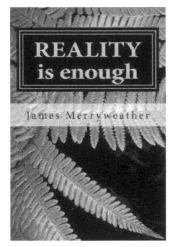

32483769R00061

Made in the USA
Charleston, SC
19 August 2014